The Technologies o

Dating to Rel

- From A to Z

(A man's guide to understanding women)

Or

"How I went from stupid to smart in just 50 years."

Or

"How I get more dates with, relationships with and proposals from
Hot Young Women at age 50 than I did at age 25."

By Mr. L. Rx

Dating To Relating – From A To Z

(A Man's Guide To Understanding Women)

By Mr. L. Rx

Dating To Relating, Inc.
4001 Kennett Pike #134
Wilmington DE 19807
302-777-1642 x 423

ISBN Number: 978-0-9822734-2-5

Copyright © 2007 Dating To Relating, Inc.

ALL RIGHTS RESERVED

No part of this book may be reproduced or utilized in any form or by any means, electronic or mechanical, including photo copying, recording or by any information storage and retrieval system, without permission in writing from the publisher.

INDEX

INTRODUCTION

I've often been asked, "what is the purpose of writing another book on dating."

Well my purpose in writing this book is two-fold.

First, there is no accurate technology on "how to meet," "how to pick up" women etc., that I am aware of. Now that doesn't mean that there are no books out there that can help guys and girls with their relationships. There are a number of books out there that contain strategies that work, but there are NO books out there that contain technologies that work- in fact, I haven't even seen a book, which addresses the technologies of dating and relating.

What is the difference between a strategy and technology? Well for the purposes of our book, let's define it as follows.

A strategy is detailed instructions on how to do something or how to approach something that if you employ (even without fully understanding it) will work a certain percentage of times.

A technology is a full understanding on all the principles of an area so that one can master the area. A technology will generate dozens of strategies each of which works under certain circumstances.

Why does anyone need a technology instead of a strategy and who would be the kind of person that would want a technology rather than a strategy?

Well there are several reasons why a person might prefer a technology to a strategy.

1) If you are just the kind of person who wants to master an area, you would prefer a technology to a strategy.

2) If you are tired of the low yield that dating strategies produce and would prefer to close 80-90% of ANY of the women you meet in ANY situation rather than 10% of the women that you meet in general circumstances you would prefer a technology to a strategy. (Actually, some strategies – some that I give you in this book – can yield as much as 80-100% results – if you apply them under certain specific conditions and with certain specific personality types. The problem is these same strategies will not work at all – 0% results – under other conditions and with other personality types.)

3) If the strategies that you have been exposed to require you to do and say things that just don't feel right, that just aren't you, then you would prefer a technology to a strategy. A technology will allow you to generate your own strategy that works for you and that you are completely comfortable with doing.

After observing the "Dating Guru" scene for many years and buying many of these products myself to sharpen my own game, I realized that none of these guys had any technology, only strategy. Moreover, when I looked at their results, their statistics were worse than mine.

I learned a lot from these typical "dating gurus." After all, anything anyone has to say on the subject is applicable to certain situations and I find that valuable. I certainly have not done everything and there are certainly many clever guys other than me who have come up with clever strategies for meeting and dating women.

So all of these guys are good guys in my opinion. They are ALL trying to help their fellow man. But there is a problem out there. There are not TECHNOLOGIES only strategies, and that is why I wrote this book.

Gurus can come up with a strategy that works from trial and error, word of mouth, watching other guys, etc. But a technology of dating and relating is a way to develop many strategies from theory and observation that are applicable across a wide variety of situations and personality types – any situation any personality type that you choose. It is a way to adjust and correct with changing times, situations, needs, etc.

Most importantly, a technology is a way to get what you want. A strategy sometimes will leave you high and dry in that department. (I learned that when I was 25 years old when I developed a strategy that worked 100% of the time on the barroom and club "beautiful tease" girls who had been my elusive fantasy challenge for years. However, after winning a number of these girls in a row, I soon learned that they were not worth the effort. Their personalities and even their physical beauty could not satisfy me.)

The second reason that I wrote this book is that I observed another big HOLE out there in the dating GURU information scene.

These DATING GURUS only talk about meeting women, picking up women, attracting women. None of these guys seem to (admittedly) know a thing about KEEPING a woman after you attract them, developing a relationship with a woman, finding a marriage partner and creating a successful marriage.

There are other guys (and girls) who write about relationships, but they don't seem to know much about dating and attracting and meeting women.

BUT THE TRUTH IS a successful relationship depends on how you go about meeting women, attracting women, qualifying women, getting to know women in the first place. They ARE NOT two different topics, as most gurus seem to make them out to be.

If you want a successful marriage or other long-term-relationship, then you had better learn first how to meet and attract women who are compatible with your own personality and needs and desires. If you do not, you won't make it a lifetime (at least not happily) with one person, no matter how good you are with the tenets of relationship technology.

So in this book, I give you the opening game, the middle game and the follow through. There is no end game, because as long as you are in a relationship there is no end – only future.

This is why I wrote this book - to fill these gaps in the informational forest of DATING and RELATING.

12/15/07

Mr. L. Rx.

FOREWORD - HOW TO USE THIS BOOK

This book contains a lot of data. Perhaps more than you will ever need or want to know.

As I've explained in the introduction, the fields or dating and relating are intertwined and related, I've tried to write this book so that the Chapters are autonomous. Occasionally they may refer to another Chapter, which if it does, you should probably look up and read.

Therefore, there are several ways you can use this book

1) You can read it from cover to cover. (Highly recommended)

2) You can use it as a reference look up a topic of your choice and read the Chapter or Chapters that cover that.

3) If you want the "meat" of my technology of meeting and picking up women then you should read Chapters 3 and 4. (Quick start)

4) If you want the "meat" of my relationship technology then you should read Chapters 8 and 9 (Quick start)

5) If you want strategies for meeting and picking up women you should read Chapters 2(c) and 6.

6) If you want strategies for relating to women then you should read Chapters 11 and 12.

Now as you read this book, if you find something that you feel you could apply to your situation, I suggest you stop right there and try it. Then come back and read a little more. Whenever you find something you can apply, stop again and apply it. Then return to read some more.

The point is to get you to apply this stuff for the betterment of your life and relationships. So if you find something that will help, put the book down and go out and do it (unless it is three in the morning and that is impractical.) The book will always be there when you return.

Mr. L. Rx

1) DATING - HOW DATING GURU'S STRATEGIES GO WRONG

THE PROBLEM WITH DATING "GURUS." The problem is simple. They only tell you how to meet and attract women. They don't tell you how to RELATE and KEEP them. WORSE yet, they don't even tell you the correct principles of MEETING women.....they tell you what worked for them.....and they tell you to do things that don't quite feel right for you......

WHY?

BECAUSE MOST GURUS HAVE NO REAL EXPERIENCE WITH MEETING A BROAD RANGE OF WOMEN AND SECURING A RELATIONSHIP WITH THEM.

Most gurus have simply discovered one technique that works (on one type of women), then do it all the time on everyone, and tell you -- it is a numbers game.

No -- It is not a numbers game - if you know what you are doing situationally, you can close 80-90% of the women that you are interested in.

When I reviewed websites before preparing this book, I couldn't believe that I actually saw gurus writing advice:

--Gurus who had no actual experience. Their advice was based on interviews!

--Gurus who were women (who don't even understand themselves) giving advice to men.

--And dozens of gurus who have techniques that *can* close women (but women that I wouldn't touch with a 10 foot pole.)

Do you want the *cream of the crop* like me or whatever you can get by closing 10-20% of whatever using a numbers game?

Numbers games aren't "technologies", they are crude strategies.

I know guys who can go into a bar and ask every women they meet very crudely, "Do you want to ####?" And guess what? Depending on the guy, if they ask 100 women or so, they'll get one to respond.

The problem with numbers games is that they make you do things that feel uncomfortable, *that aren't quite you*...and they don't work on the women you really want!!!

2) DIFFERENT MEN LIKE DIFFERENT WOMEN -- DIFFERENT WOMEN REQUIRE DIFFERENT STRATEGIES

The problem is, there are different TYPES of men. And different types of men like different types of women. Different types of women require different strategies for each type. And I'm here to tell you all of them.

IF YOU WANT GOOD ADVICE, YOU SHOULD SEEK OUT SOMEONE WHO HAS ACTUALLY DONE IT AND LEARN FROM THEM.

I HAVE DONE IT ALL!

--I have met and maintained relationships with a broad variety of different women.

--I have successfully met women (and developed relationships with them)

in bars
in clubs
naturally -- on the street, in the store, etc.
online
through newspaper and voice mail advertising through friends

--I have gone on over 700 dates with different women in one year.

--I have had a marriage last 12 years without ever cheating on my wife.

--I have had a monogamous relationship with a girlfriend for 7 years without ever cheating on her.

--I have had multiple long term sexual relationships with as many as 10 women at once without hiding my intentions or lying to any one of them.

--I have gone to bars and clubs and gotten laid by one-nighters every night for months on end.

--I have gotten laid by a different woman every night of the week for months on end.

--I have manipulated the manipulators (you know, p***** teasers)who were out to use me. (Yes, of course, I got sex, but it wasn't very good)

--I have gone to strip clubs and had the strippers ask me out! Then take me home and have sex with me.

--I have had several women ask me to father their child - no strings attached.

--I could go on and on.

WHO AM I? Let me introduce myself. I am Mr. L. RX (Why Mr. L. RX? Well, I would rather remain anonymous. I am not into being famous. I do not have to prove anything to anyone; I would just like to help a few guys out by giving them CORRECT information on women.)

WHAT MAKES ME QUALIFIED TO BE AN EXPERT ON DATING AND RELATING?

My Credentials

Well, I am 54 years old. and though at 20 I couldn't even get a girlfriend, I currently have 6 long term (2-5 years) sexual/romantic relationships going with younger women (Ages 22, *25,* 26, 27, 30, and 40.) **NO, I AM NOT A PLAYER.** I was married 12 years and never cheated on my wife. If I am in a committed relationship, I don't cheat. BUT in-between committed relationships, I am looking. And I feel I have the right to date and have sex with as many women as I want, as long as I am HONEST with them about it and practice safe sex.

IT TOOK ME 50 YEARS but I finally got to understand and become very successful with women.

MY STATISTICS of SUCCESS

Teenager, 0 dates. Virgin until 19. Lost my virginity to **a** legal whore in Nevada. Although considered "hot" by most women, once they met me I blew them away. First girlfriend by 20. I was married by 22, but had a miserable marriage and was divorced by *25.* BUT....

BY 25 ½, I had learned how to get laid *5* times a week in bars and clubs. Things I learned from these experiences culminated in me becoming a very good lover, and getting married again at 31 to a 19-year-old woman.... But I was divorced again by 42. BUT...

BY 43 ½, I had learned how to get 2 dates a day with personal ads. I had over 700 dates in my first year alone. This culminated in me meeting the best sexual partner I had ever had (and I had had quite a few) which resulted in a 7-year relationship, but by 50 this was over too (not because of the sex- it was hot even after we broke up) but...

BY 52, I had learned how to get and maintain long term multiple sexual relationship **without lying to anyone.** (I usually have about 6-10 younger (19-40) sexual partners that I see once a week or once every other week, or once a month, depending on MY interest level. Most of these relationships I had maintained for years. Most of the relationships I had developed between 48 and 50 have been maintained for *5* years, others 2 or 3 or 4 years.)

NOW at 54, I feel complete in my knowledge, I can meet women anywhere:-- in a club, on the Internet, in personal ads, through friends, and on the street. If I want, I can close about 90% of the qualified women I meet for long term sexual relationship or marriage. Once married, I am a good honest man that knows how to treat a woman, emotionally and sexually. I am not currently married (though I have had about 4 proposals and 4 girls who would marry me in an instant if I asked), because I won't settle for anything less than a, beautiful, classy, intelligent and emotionally mature woman, that has a great family and friends, knows what she wants to do with her life exactly, and has many, many things in common with me. (Unfortunately as of this writing, I haven't found her yet.)

In other words, I have the beginning game, middle game and the follow through all down.

AND though there is a lot of good information and good guys (like David DeAngelo, David M., Mystery, etc.) teaching guys stuff in seminars, books, private coaching, etc. They are all missing little pieces of the truth. Their techniques work, but only with a certain kind of woman. "Cocky and Funny", for example, doesn't generally work on the classy, intelligent women that I like. And sure Mystery's techniques work on bar and club women (I know his techniques work, because I did almost exactly the same thing in 1978 when I got laid in clubs *5* times a week by "one night stands".) but bar and club women again aren't the classy intelligent women that I LIKE.... **And perhaps you are like me**...

MORE OF MY STORY

When I was a young man. I was simply hot. I never chased women. Women chased me. I had experiences that guys typically didn't have. Girls stopped their cars and tried to pick me up, girls whistled at me. Younger girls who knew me in school, upon turning 18 usually, would confess that they had a crush on me all their lives. Girls would approach me on the beach and tell me I was the hottest guy on the beach...one girl even stopped the elevator mid-floor and told me I wasn't getting off until I kissed her....

BUT-- don't go anywhere, just because I was HOT doesn't mean I got women. I just got approached all the time. As SOON AS I OPENED MY MOUTH (or shortly thereafter), **I LOST THEM. THEY WOULD TELL ME I WAS NUTS, AND RUN AWAY**. I didn't quite understand it then, but I DO NOW.

SOMEHOW, I managed to get married by 22, to my first girlfriend (She was NUTS too), and had a terrible marriage, and got divorced

When I was *25 (1978)* after a failed marriage, I decided to START LEARNING, I hung out in bars 24/7 until I figured out "how to get laid." It took me 3 months. After 3 months **I could go out *7* days a week and get laid *5* of those days by "one nighters" that I liked.**

What I learned at this time was that, although I was good looking, that didn't matter. **I became successful by learning what to say to women.**

I eventually got married again to a woman who was 19 when I was 31. We were married 12 years and had 2 children. When we broke up, I was 42.

Now when I became single again at 42, I was not as good looking as the teenage to 30-year-old version of myself. I was still trim and in good physical shape and didn't quite look my true age, but I was balding and knew I couldn't compete with a hot *25* year old on sheer looks.

What I soon was to learn, however, is that **it doesn't hurt to have "good looks" but it is not really important**. All it gets you is attention. **There are other ways to get a woman's attention.** MONEY, good conversation, personality, and technique are some that come to mind.

What I was soon to learn was that an Older, Balder version of me could get more young women...and keep them... than the Younger, Hotter Version of me ever could.

I DECIDED TO LEARN SOME MORE. I started exploring personal ads, which were big at the time. Within about 3 months again I was routinely going on 2 dates a day (YES A DAY) for about a little over a year. That's right I had over 700 dates in one year alone. Believe me, it was a part time job. After about 13 months of this, I settled down with one woman I met and she became my girlfriend -- after about 3 months of dating. I lost interest in all other women and in meeting new women. I had a monogamous relationship with her and was faithful for 7 years to her.

WHEN I BROKE UP WITH HER, (at age *50)* I decided to learn the rest of the things I still didn't know to really master the area. I explored personal ads some more, Internet dating, and meeting people on the streets and through friends.

Within about 3 months again, **I learned how to have multiple sexual partners/friends (notice I don't use the term Girlfriend) without LYING.** I have had as many as 10 sexual partners/friends at one time (but I found this a little exhausting) and prefer to have about 6 sexual partners friends and see about 3 or 4 of them a week, using my other nights to continue my search for the ideal /marriage partner.

Though I haven't found my ideal marriage partner yet, it is because I have become very picky, because I won't settle for anything less than a beautiful, classy, intelligent and emotionally mature woman, that has a great family and friends, knows what she wants to do with her life exactly, and has many, many things in common with me.

I must say I am as content as a single guy could be. And I am more successful with women now at 54 then I have ever been. (And it is with the same age group that I have always been interested in 18-35) My multiple partners kind of combine into one ideal woman, but of course... in the final analysis... **I really am a monogamous man and would rather be married....**

But TODAY I am here to help you.

In this BOOK - you will learn how to:

- **MEET any type of women in any TYPE of situation**

- Use PICK UP lines and PICK UP technique laid out for different situations

- Develop your own PICK UP lines and PICK UP technique from the principles you learn

- Exact techniques for approaching different types of women and establishing a relationship.

- How to understand how different types of women think and how to approach each type.

- How to approach women without feeling uncomfortable

- What does feet have to do with it? That's right-- how feet can be a guide to SANITY in meeting and relating to women.

- Learning how to understand and use subtle and gradient communications that women use.

- How to get women to approach you, and make the moves on you first.

- How to prospect and qualify - that's right guys, we are salesmen!

- How to reject girls - let them down easy. Get use to it. You'll have so many girls, you'll have to let a few of them go!

- How to define what your ideal woman is so you know what you are prospecting for.

- Exact techniques for meeting women in different settings -- bars, street, stores, etc.

- How to establish "Future" with a woman. Relationships start here.

- How to establish "Future" with a woman walking down the street, in the mall, etc.

- Exact techniques for what to do on the first date so you don't blow it.

- Exact techniques for what to do on the 2nd, 3rd, 4th, 5th, etc. dates so you don't blow it.

And once you make it that far I'll even tell you how to develop your budding relationship.

Relationships - The Problem With Dating "Gurus"

The problem is simple. They only tell you how to meet and attract women. They don't tell you how to RELATE and KEEP them.

Relationships - what a topic to tackle. Even the mightiest of dating gurus don't tackle that one. Why? Because it is a lot more complicated then just getting someone to meet you, hang out with you a few times, etc.

A lot of the principles that go into a successful relationship for a man, are the same principles that are required when trying to attract and/or meet women.

First of all, there are different types of relationships that people have. Among the types of sexual relationships men and women have are:

Prostitution (pay for sex)
One night stands
Friends with privileges
Dating with casual sex
Lovers only.
Arrangements (You take care of me, I'll take care of you)
Multiple Lovers
Swinging
Affairs (cheating on someone)
Girlfriend/Boyfriend
Living together
Marriage.
Divorce (Yes, some people even have sex after marriage, sort of friends with privileges phase again.)

So the first question we have to ask when talking about relationships is "What Kind" of relationship. There are different rules and different procedures for establishing each kind of relationship.

But before we get too far down that direction, let's also remember there are different personality types for both men and women. Different personalities types want different things out of a relationship, they also interact differently -- some compatibly, some boringly, others not so compatibly.

THROW that on top of the different types of relationships and you already have a complicated mess. NO WONDER the DATING GURUS don't tackle this stuff! It is hard to generalize about relationships because the complexities of the above interactions make it a vastly complicated subject.

It takes a guy with REAL EXPERIENCE with ALL KINDS of different relationships and all kinds of different personalities, and a guy who is old enough for his own personality to have undergone various changes throughout his life, to even be half-way qualified to shed some light on this subject.

That is where I come in - Been there. Done that.

And lucky for you, I understand it and can explain it. (I'm not the only guy who has been there and done that, but I may be one of the few who understands it and can explain it SITUATIONALLY and in DETAIL.

EVERYTHING is SITUATIONAL when it comes to meeting and relating to women. Different personalities (yours and the woman's) and different types of relationships require a complexity of different strategies.

Thus, you can see it evolves that the strategies or technologies of meeting and relating to women are numerous and complex themselves, because basically you need a different strategy for EACH DIFFERENT SITUATION you find yourself in. Some strategies appear to be the exact opposite of other strategies. (See Chapter 2 (c) for an example of this.)

THIS is what most DATING GURUS don't tell you. They learn one strategy that works in one situation, tell you about it and then tell you it is a numbers game.

IT IS NOT A NUMBERS GAME! 90% of the women I target, I get a date with. 90% of the women I get a first date with, I get and second and third if I want. 99% of the women who go out with me on a second date with me want a relationship with me. 99% of the women I go out with who actually want to get married, want to marry me after anywhere from 3 dates (the crazy ones) to a year.

DOES THIS MEAN I am saying you or I can get ANY GIRL he wants. No. I am not saying that. (Although it is possible and I show you "how" in this book under the section on Seduction!) What I am saying is that if you learn the situational technologies of how to meet and relate to women, and you qualify prospects (like any good salesman) - and you will find there are lots of qualified prospects-- you will close a large percentage of them if you use the techniques I will be teaching you. (When I say CLOSE, I mean that the girl wants a second date with you. I don't mean that you actually have to go out with 90% of the girls you meet on a second date. 90% of the girls I meet want to go out on a second date with me. However, I only want to go out with about 5% of the girls I meet- not because they are not pretty but because I am beyond that - all the girls I date are pretty, but I am looking for a certain personality that is a good prospect for marriage and I won't settle for anything less.)

Though I will go into each of these complex interactions of relationships and personalities elsewhere, for now, let us stay focused for the moment on the commonalities we find in any of the above relationships.

Just as in music, there may be vast difference between genres such a Rap, Country and Western, Pop, and Rock. The differences are so vast that if you were an artist and you approached performing one genre the exact same way you did another- you would be a big time loser. However, still, there are commonalities in music that underlie and are true for all of these genres. Knowing the basics would make you a good musician/performer and give you an ability to cross genre and do well modifying and adding to your basics situationally as the genre demanded.

So let me recap, There are a multitude of relationships. Personality is not a constant for men or women. These two factors generate a huge amount of different strategies or technologies of meeting and relating to women.

BUT, Lucky for you the Commonalities of relating to people are MUCH MORE IMPORTANT than the situational variables. Because the big mistakes you make in relating to people and women are violating BASIC common principles. If you are a guy and you find yourself unable to develop a relationship with ANY woman. I guarantee you are violating basic common principles. If you can have relationships with some women, but can't understand others or the kind you would like to understand, you are violating situational principles.

Here is another way of saying it:

If women are constantly breaking up with you, you are violating basic common principles of relating.

If you are constantly breaking up with women, you are violating situational common principles.

In either case, this book will help you with relationships.

Here are a few of the things you will learn from it:

> **-How to step-by-step develop a relationship. How to meet women and what to do on dates 1, 2, 3, 4, 5, etc.**
>
> **-How to avoid the mistakes guys make in the early stages of dating. The mistakes that "doom" a relationship.**
>
> **-The best defense against having a bad relationship. - perspective -- the ability to have plenty of women to chose from.**
>
> **-How to have 3-5 women who want to marry you BEFORE you make a decision.**

-How to prospect for and qualify women. YES, just like a salesman, you need to qualify women to get the kind of woman who is best for you and that you can relate to effortlessly.

-How to get women to do what you want without having to bitch at them.

-How to communicate to a woman in ways that she will understand.

-What to communicate to women about.

-When to communicate to a woman.

-How to understand what women are really saying.

-How to know what your woman really wants.

-How to have multiple relationships, arrangements, lovers and other non-traditional relationships.

-How to have multiple relationships without lying to anyone.

-How to get a woman to have the kind of relationship YOU want to have without having to lie to her.

-How NOT to lose your soul (integrity) just for a little SEX!

-How to seduce a woman. (How to get and keep any woman you want!)

-How to develop and maintain Romance in a relationship forever!

-How to be a good lover! (how to satisfy women in bed)

-How to have a beautiful, loving relationship with one woman the rest of your life!

Examples of Strategies and How Different Personalities Can Require Completely Opposite Strategies

The mistake the Dating Gurus make is that women are different. The Dating Gurus have all developed "systems" that work. They work on a certain type of women.... but not ALL women. **WHY?** There is not one system that works on all types of women. There are different types of women and different strategies that work on these different types. Some strategies are exactly the opposite of others.

For example, when I was a young and stupid, 25 or so, I worked the bar scene every day for six months straight. I developed a strategy very similar to the "Mystery" system, which was pretty much 100% effective with a certain type of girl (beautiful women who toyed with and teased men). But, there were other kinds of girls in the bar, and truth be told the kind of women that the "Mystery" type technique works on, didn't satisfy me emotionally or physically. Three of the groups I classified women into in those days were: "Love-Girls," "regular women," and "the beautiful teases." The beautiful Teases gave most guys the most problems, the regular women were the hardest, and the Love Girls were the easiest (if you had technique and some balls) and were the most satisfying emotionally and were the best lovers physically.

EXAMPLES

Let me give you some concrete examples of what I am talking about. Here is what I did 25 years a go in the bars.

First of all I stood around for about a month and did nothing. I was scared shitless. I had just gotten divorced (from a wife who was also my first girl friend) and I was shy and didn't have much experience with women.

Love Girls: So for the first month I just stood around and observed. One of the things I observed early on was Love Girls. Love Girls were women who came into the bar usually late (about 11 or 12) and basically they were looking to get laid. They were great looking, confident women. They always walked in alone (NOT with a girl friend) and they walked slowly and sexily through the club. They looked every man in their path directly in the eyes, but I observed the typical guy would get shy and embarrassed and would look away. He would then gulp down some alcohol and I could see him trying to build up his courage to go back at her. However, the Love Girls would move on and if no guy did the right thing she would walk through the club and then LEAVE. (She wanted to get laid and wasn't going to waste time with a bunch of losers. She would just move on to the next club.)

Every once in a while, however, I would notice some guy would walk up to one of these Love Girls as she walked buy and simply ask her to dance. "Would you like to dance?" Nothing more and nothing less. I then noticed whenever this happened the "Love Girl" would always say "Yes" no matter what the guy looked like and then they would go out on the dance floor and dance for half and hour or so, then they would leave together.

So after a few observations, I tried it. I walked right up to a Love Girl and said "Would you like to dance?" she said "Yes" We danced for a while, definitely in the sex groove, then I asked her if she wanted to go to my place. Again, she said, "yes." We went to my place and of course had sex.

Not only did it work with the first "Love Girl", but it worked over and over again. All I had to do was SPOT a love girl-- by her characteristic walk, dress, attitude, confront, etc. then the rest was easy. Then I got even smarter when I spotted this band one day. There were a dozen or so Love Girls in the audience. But NOW they were REALLY horny because they all thought this band was real sexy. Well this time, I just turned to the girl behind me who was real hot and sexy, and with out a word I just started kissing her (remember this was the 70's before AIDS. So I wouldn't do and wouldn't suggest stuff like this now. I am just using it for illustration PURPOSES.) She kissed me back, and after a few moment of making out, without a word, I took her hand and we went out side to the parking lot, got in my car, and had sex right there, then came back into the club, when we were done. I don't know and never even asked her name.

After that, I made a point of getting this band's schedule and started following them. Worked Like a charm. A number of years later I also found that if I went to the bars that had the male stripper shows for girls only, right after the show was over, there were always a bunch of horny Love Girls on the spot no fail.

The Beautiful Tease: Another observation I made over the course of time were the beautiful women, who purposely teased men. They flirted with you, but when you went over to hit on them, they would eventually go cold, after a while they would totally ignore you. This tease left you totally confused, after all, how many women flirt with you, hit up on you? She had to like you, right? Well, these girls always had a cadre of frustrated men following them wherever they went, kissing their asses and confused.

I began to notice that the only guys who ever left with these teases, or ended up dating them, were the guys who totally ignored them, who seemed like they could care less, then one day I just got *it.* It came to me in a brainstorm. I realized that you had to ignore a tease, get her to hit on you and keep her hitting on you all the way into bed by continuing to ignore her. But the question was: How do you communicate to some one you are ignoring? Well the answer ended up in a technique similar to what "Mystery" uses now a day. I would simply walk over to one of theses hot teases, position myself right next to her (but not looking at her--sort of shoulder to shoulder--close enough that she could hear me but not close enough that she would take my position as showing any interest in her) and then I would wait for another hot girl to walk by or close. As soon as one did, I would shake my head as if to myself, and mutter some comment such as, "Is she hot or what?" or "Wow."

No matter what I said it was always a comment on how hot the girl who walked by was. I would always end the comment by looking at the tease, as if she were just some stranger, who I was randomly expressing my delight in "the girl who just walked by" to. WITHOUT FAIL, the tease would very shortly always then tell me in one way or another that guys do to her what I just did to this other girl ALL the time.

(NOW HERE IS THE CLOSE) I would look at her like she was a little nuts, like she wasn't hot at all, but would say very politely (as if feigning politeness) "Really" or some such comment to get her to talk some more. (Of course they would always go on and on at this point trying to convince me how hot they were, and after 15-30 minutes or so, I would say something like "Look, maybe you ARE a good looking woman, it's just perhaps hard for me to see it because you are definitely NOT my type" (I would then describe my type to be the opposite of whatever they were. If they were blonde, I liked brunettes. If they had big ones, I liked little ones, etc.) Then I would say, "But did you ever consider that perhaps men like you NOT for the way you look, but for your personality, because after listening to you here for awhile, I THINK you have a great personality and maybe that is why men like you.

After those words, the Tease was mine. They would invariably say. "Oh my god, I have never met a guy like you in my life. I can't believe you. I have never had a guy say he likes my personality. (Rightfully so, because they were usually perceived by men as cold bitches.) You are so interesting...

From that point, the girl would invite me out, and generally increase the gradient of flirting and teasing to get a reaction out of me as she typically got from all those other men, and when she didn't get the reaction, she would up the ante of flirting, until she eventually, jumped me (had sex with me) to get a reaction. (It usually took 3 dates.) But, of course, I knew from months of observation, that if I ever admitted I was attracted to her, if, I ever took the lead and hit on her, or let her know that I was really attracted to her and was lying, it would be over. So, I never did. Instead, I only complimented her personality, and if I said anything about her physically, I always did it as if I was being polite and trying not to hurt her feelings. Or I would say something that gave her a sense of progress (the idea that they were winning me over) but never a full compliment--something like "You are still not my type, but you are looking more attractive to me then when I first met you. Who knows, maybe I COULD see you as totally beautiful some day. "Eventually, as I said, they would tease me all the way into bed. And even after sex, when they asked me "Was it good" I would simply respond " it was Ok...but that is not important, what is important is that you are a great person, and I really like you." (Now this was never hard to do, because Teases without variation, were the worse lovers as a group that I ever met.)

After a while, I got to understand what was really going on with these girls and why they did what they did. They were all beautiful girls who were made to feel unconfident as children. They were all told they were ugly and such things, when they in fact weren't. So they grew up with low self-esteem and were actually very afraid of men. Somewhere along the line, however, they learned that men reacted well to them and that they could get men to do anything they wanted by flirting with them. In their minds, they still did not think men did this because they were good looking; they just thought men did it because men were horny and easy to manipulate. So, when they flirt with a man, and the man reaches and aggresses back, these girls basically get scared and run away. They are working on their self-confidence, however, that is why they are in the bar every day or every weekend. And when I didn't aggress against them sexually, but told them I liked them, I gave them a safe zone. They weren't afraid of me. So they raised the bar and tried to "win me over" so to speak. Winning me over, made them feel better about themselves. And of course got me laid. This strategy worked 100% of the time.

Then there were the regular girls; I use to call them **GRADIENT GIRLS.** I called them that because after a lot of observations I noticed there was a gradient scale of sexual reach or interest. Here it is:

First, there is negative sexual talk. (This is talking about not having sex, or not wanting to have sex, or talking about someone else who is into sex as creepy, disgusting, or characterizing them in some other negative way, etc. This is the lowest form of sexual interest someone can show you. Because they still ARE talking about sex. And they are talking about it with YOU. People who really aren't interested in sex or you don't bring it up at all, and really don't get "into it" if you bring it up. I learned about this one day, when I was driving a fellow student home from college. She invited me up to her apartment, but quickly informed me that I couldn't have sex with her. Since, I had shown her no sexual interest, and since I really wasn't interested, I found this rather odd. A few weeks later, she seduced me. She got me to have sex with her when I didn't want to and wasn't really attracted to her. This is when I put it all together. She was attracted to me from the very first. And her negative comment about "not having sex" was the level at which she began her sexual flirting.)
Then positive sexual talk.
Then Eye Contact
Then slight brief touching
Then extended touching.
Then kissing,
Petting,
Heavy petting,
Intercourse.

Now most people think sexual interest starts with positive sexual talk, but it doesn't. And the funny thing about this gradient scale is that you have to match the level the other person is at or you can lose a prospect very quickly. So if a girl is into flirting at "negative sexual talk" and you try to come on her at "positive sexual talk" you will lose her.

Now most of your regular girls hanging out in clubs, whether with or without girlfriends, have a negative view towards guys. They think guys who are there just want sex, etc. And they are probably right. So the way I would come on to a regular girl in a club, was simple. I would stand next to her (similar to the Tease Girl above) and wait for some guy to hit on some girls in a stupid way that confirms what most girls thinks about guys. I would then make a comment about how stupid that was, etc. sort of out loud to myself or whomever was around (sort of like I did with the Tease Girl) ending by looking at her in disbelief. She would then chime in very quickly about how stupid it was, and from there I would lead the conversation into a negative "sex talk" about how I hated clubs, hated all the games and meat market stuff that goes on, etc. This would usually go on for about 15-30 minutes and then she would invariably say the magic words: **"But you are different"** to which I would reply "Yeah, you are different too." From there it could go in many directions depending on the girls. We might dance, or continue in an engaging conversation, but now the conversation was into positive sexual talk, from there we would start with the little touches etc, and eventually it would lead to making out, petting, heavy petting, kissing, etc.

Now none of these techniques are "Cocky and Funny" or any such, and by the way Cocky and Funny does work on a small band of girls in the club (and in life) too. I would label them the Boredom girls.

But here is the principal behind Cocky and Funny and the Love Girl, Tease Girl and Regular Girl techniques. And that principal is not to be "cocky and Funny" but rather to be "Interesting and Unique."

You see the guy who has the balls to walk up to and confront the horny "Love Girl" is interesting and unique to her because most guys are too scared to do it. But he is definitely Not Cocky and Funny. He only has to open his mouth and confidently ask her to dance. The guy who tells the "Tease Girl" she's not that hot, but has a good personality is "interesting and Unique" to her, because ALL guys reach at these girls and tell then how beautiful they are. The guy who can dish out negative sex talk to a "Regular Girl" is interesting and Unique" to her because she never finds guys like this in the club. And of course the Boredom Girls, who get guy after guy after guy hitting on them and kissing their ass find "Cocky and Funny" totally interesting and Unique. Boredom girls are a kind of random, casual, and pointless-talk band of girl, and Cocky and Funny is random and pointless talk. The other techniques are more directed.

There are other types of girls too, and combination of types. We will go over some of these others in later Chapters.

Some techniques are quick and easy and some techniques are pure seduction and can take a very long time. We will also go over some of these in later Chapters.

3) TWO BASIC PROBLEMS

What Guys Do Wrong

We all know there are differences between men and women - mentally, physically, and emotionally.

There are guys that don't get the basic differences between men and women, and there are women who likewise don't understand men. The basic error is to think that the opposite sex thinks like you do, or to get upset when we realize that they don't.

So let me help some of you guys by giving you the basic relevant differences between men and women. When I say, "relevant", I mean relevant to our "dating" and "relationship" issues. If you understand these basic differences, you will improve your ability to be successful at dating and relating to women.

I saw a show on Discovery Channel about a year ago. Very educational. Went over these basic male/female "mental and physical" differences. Whether this stuff is true or not, whether the differences are learned or not, I don't know. Many studies find no differences between men and women on lots of variables like cognitive ability, etc.

Interesting show, though. Goes back to the basic difference that men have a bigger heart than women do. Pumps more blood and that's why we are basically bigger, stronger and faster than women.

But that is a given. Every guy knows we are bigger, stronger and faster than women, even if they don't know why.

The most interesting thing that was revealed on this Discovery show, however, had to do with perception. Women and men were shown a picture for a fraction of a second. Men, on the average, couldn't identify what the picture was, whereas women could not only tell you what it was - a face - but they could even tell you the emotion on the face.

We will get back to that one in a minute.

Another important physical difference is an obvious one - a woman's ability to bear children.

Now somehow or another (either learned, environmental, hormonal, or whatever) this ability leads to another big difference between men and women.

Going back to the evolution of our species, it is easy to see that women - already not as big or strong as men - were at a further physical disadvantage to men during pregnancy. Especially at the later stages of pregnancy, women are more susceptible to the difference in strength and speed. Then after a woman gives birth, she has an even weaker body to take care of in addition to hers - a child.

So it is not hard to see why a woman came to need, want or "value" the protection of the stronger gender - the protection of a man. Perhaps in a "caveman" society, women wanted the "biggest and baddest" dinosaur killer around. In modern times, however, protection can be not only physical, but also mental, emotional, financial, etc.

Obviously there are dozens if not hundreds of more differences between men and women, but it is the above two differences that could be said to have some "physical" basis that produce the most important differences between men and women for our purposes of understanding dating and relating.

How does this need for "protection" affect a woman in our modern day dating and relating environment?

The majority of women (I'd estimate 66%) aren't looking for the hottest, cutest, man around when it comes to dating and relating. There are looking for "chemistry" and that "chemistry" is usually some form of mental, emotional, or physical protection whether "conscious" or "sub-conscious." Women like men who can make them feel "safe" on some basic instinctual level.

The majority of men (again, I'd estimate 66%) are the opposite. They are looking for the hottest, cutest girl that they can get. When it comes to dating and relating this is what men are looking for first and foremost.

How do I apply this knowledge of these differences in a dating and relating environment? Well, I actually don't apply this one to women much. It is something that I apply to myself.

When I am 50 years old and going after that hot young 25-year-old girl, I'm not worried about how "hot" I look compared to young men. I just know that I can make any woman (regardless of age) feel safer around me than most of my competition (regardless of age.)

Even if a woman "thinks" she likes cute guys, I know I can get to her "basic instinct." I can make her feel more safe and protected around me than most other guys.

Then throw in the fact that I know more about sexual pleasure than most young guys, and I can take her to nicer places than most young guys and you see, after a while, it really isn't a competition - no matter how the woman feels at first.

How can you apply this? The same way I do. It is the great equalizer. No matter what you look like. No matter if you are fat, bald, or just plain ugly - when it comes to women, it really doesn't matter. And as a guy you have to get that. Women aren't like us. They aren't looking for the cutest guy around. Know this, and you will have the confidence to go after any woman. And if you apply the rest of the stuff I teach you, you have a chance of getting her.

If you are in a relationship, you can apply this too. Women want to feel safe around you. Is it always physical safety? No. But some girls do like big men because of the appeal to this basics instinct. In our society, however, safety is more often "emotional safety", "mental safety" more than physical safety.

So don't be stupid. Make your woman feel safe.

This basic, basic instinct cuts across all personality types, although it may be expressed differently with a different personality type.

Going back to my examples that I discussed in Chapter 2 (c) about the barroom personality types, You can see the "Love Girl" felt safe with a guy who was confident enough to walk up to her and ask her to dance.

The Gradient Girls felt "safe' after I gradiently assured them that I wasn't the "jerk" they were expecting.

And the Beautiful Teases definitely felt "safe" with a guy who seduced them into hitting on him, rather than hitting on them like most guys.

You see my strategies, though vastly different for each type of girl, made each of these girls feel safe. It appealed to their basic instinct - and not one of these girls cared what I looked like.

And that is the thing to remember, guys, for women, it is not about what you look like. It is about how you make them feel when they are with you.

For us guys the basic instinct is to get the hottest and best looking chick you can get to hang on your arm. It is about showing off your conquest to other guys. We do not need women to protect us. We need a trophy. We need bragging rights in the locker room.

Why? Well because in modern society maybe some other guy is bigger, stronger, and "badder" than you physically, but you know damn well, not matter how little, or stupid or average you are, if you got a hotter girl than he has, you'll get his respect. (As long as he is not a "caveman" who tries to beat the crap out of you and take her away!)

So we apply the knowledge of this difference to ourselves.

It is the second difference that I mentioned above however, that we apply to women.

Women could see a face and an emotion when shown a picture for a fraction of a second. Whereas men could not even tell it was a face, much less get the emotion.

Whether learned or some sort of natural physical ability, women are much more perceptive than men are. If you want to be successful in dating and relating to women, you have to know this about them.

A whole world of perception exists for women that most men just do not see. But personally I think it is mainly learned behavior on the part of men, because though I started out more stupid and more dumb, more blind and more ignorant than most men, I have learned to be as equally perceptive as most women that I now meet.

Now this is the biggie! If you can learn this one, it will remarkably change your ability to deal with women successfully. Why? Because how can you successfully deal with or handle something, you can't even see? You have to train yourself to see it first, then you can easily deal with it.

What made women more perceptive? Perhaps it is because of their traditional role of caring for children - having to be attentive, having to know what every little subtle move, sound, look from an infant or child means.

Or maybe it has to do with the fact that physically their bodies are more subtle in communicating sexual stimulation than men's. A woman doesn't get turned on instantly like a man does most of the time. Her signals are a number of successive subtle clues that lead her to the same place that a man arrives at in one fell swoop.

Whatever the reason, women are more perceptive, BUT and that is a big BUT, men can learn to be just as perceptive. (See the next Chapter)

Just so you know, it is not like women have this huge thing going on that they aren't telling us about. In fact, they tell us all the time. It just that we aren't listening and seeing what they are telling and showing us.

So train yourself. Read the Chapter on gradients, that is a good start. Talk to women. Ask them what they think about stuff, what they perceive. Be open to seeing things. Viewpoints that you never saw before. Don't argue with them. It isn't a matter of right and wrong. It is a matter of learning to see what women see.

It is true for them. It doesn't matter if it is not true for you. You are just trying to see what they see. When you can do this, then you will understand women better.

Again, I refer you to my old Barroom types for analogies. When I saw that the "Love Girl" was looking for confidence in a man, I knew what to show her. When I saw the gradient girl was looking for assurance that a man in a bar wasn't a "jerk" I knew what to show her. When I saw that the Beautiful Tease was looking for someone she could talk to who wouldn't come onto her (despite her flirting) I knew what to show her.

So the first step in improving your perception and understanding women, is try to see things from a woman's perspective, rather than from your own.

You see there aren't that many real differences between men and women's personality. It is situational. Put yourself in a woman's situation and you would probably think just like she does. Demean her way of thinking, make fun of it and yeah, you'll have good stories to tell all your other loser guy friends, but you won't have many women.

So let's take an example. What do you do if you are like most guys when you see a hot babe walking down the street?

Well again that is situational, it depends on your personality. Let's just break it down into two personality types for the sake of our discussion: aggressive vs. shy or passive guys. And then let's take the aggressive guy as our example.

The aggressive guy walks up to the girl and depending on his experience and technique he tries to talk to her in some way. But no matter his experience, chances are within a few minutes he is going to tell her she is the "hottest babe he has ever seen" in one way or another.

Ask any hot woman you know. Happens about 99% of the time.

Ok. Now most aggressive guys just look at this situation from their own point of view. They like her. They want her. They must talk to her or there is NO chance. They must tell her "I like her." So she knows.

Now let's put ourselves in her position for a minute. Look at it from her perspective. If she is really, really hot she probably gets hit up on 1-20 times a day depending on whether she is in a populated environment or not.

So let's say she works in a big city and gets hit on about 5 times a day. That means she has heard your basic "line" at least 35 times this week and 140+ times this month, and 1500+ times this year. Depending on how old she is, it could be the 10,000 th time she has experienced such a "come on" (if she is in her mid twenties).

Now maybe she was impressed with some cute guy and she indulged herself when she was 15, when she heard the line for the first time, but she subsequently learned that was a mistake and would never do that again. She has that basic instinct going and she just wants someone to make her feel emotionally and mentally safe.

She would like to meet some guy who "really" likes her for her "personality." She would recognize her prince charming because he wouldn't be stupid enough to say he was in "love" with her just by looking at her. He would be the type of guy who would want to get to know her first, and after finding out they had things in common and got along, he would fall in love with her over time.

Now after 10,000 guys all saying the same thing, she pretty much doesn't believe her prince charming even exists, and if he does, she would certainly never meet him on the street.

So what would impress her? What would break the pattern?

A guy who would show interest in her. (Talk to her.) But not say he was in love or how hot she was (because even though her looks get his attention, he could only "fall in love" with someone who had the right personality.) Instead he would probably talk to her in a way to qualify her (find out if she has similar interests, etc.) and then make up some excuse to check her out further with no commitment, rather than ask her out on a date. (Girls like it and find it extremely romantic when they know a guy is subtly checking them out.)

Now if a guy did this, he would be different from all of those other 10,000 guys and would probably walk away with her phone number (and her intention to actually answer the call or return the call) if he wanted to.

You see girls are perceptive. Girls know that when a guy walks up to a girl he doesn't know and asks her out on a date, his ONLY possible motive is sex. WHY? He has no other data. He doesn't know anything else about her other than how she looks.

Girls want to check you out. You may be cute, but they still want to check you out and make sure you have that "protection" factor.

Now, again, this is situational. This applies to HOT, HOT girls. If a girl is ugly, put yourself in her shoes. She NEVER gets guys hitting on her, and if one did, she'd probably jump in bed with them in two seconds flat.

But again, there are different personalities. A happy ugly girl, an angry ugly girl, and a sad ugly girl would all respond differently and have to be approached differently. The happy ugly girl would be the one who would jump in bed with you the quickest.

So in summary, the two things to remember here are that the differences between men and women that apply to dating and relationships have to do with 1) a woman's basic instinct is to want protection from a man; to feel mentally, emotionally, or physically safe around a man. 2) Women perceive things differently than men. They see more, and they see gradients that men usually don't see, but that men can train themselves to see. Remember, both of these are more important than his looks.

The first step in training, is to put yourself in a woman's' position when you are approaching her or relating to her. See things situationally as she would see them, and you may get some good clues on how to approach and/or relate to women and you will begin to realize that women aren't so different from men. They just find themselves in different situations.

Men are mostly the aggressors, and women are mostly the recipients of their attention. (Notice I didn't say passive.) That is a big situational difference. If you don't believe me try selling door-to-door (aggressive) as opposed to working as a sale clerk (passive) behind the counter at J.C. Penny's for a while.

What People Do Wrong

Sometimes we get confused by our lack of understanding of the opposite sex to the point that we want to explain everything with the viewpoint "Women are from Venus and Men are from Mars."

It may very well be that men and women have vastly different emotional and mental viewpoints on life, as discussed in the last Chapter, but it is my experience and contention that those vast differences are actually pretty easy to understand.

The real problem in dating and relating is that there are happy Venusians, sad Venusians, angry Venusians, sarcastic Venusians, intelligent Venusians, and stupid Venusians. And of course the same goes for Martians.

The point is there is more personality difference and variation between a happy Venusian and a sad Venusian then there is between Venusians and Martians in general.

On top of that is the additional problem that people have "social" personalities. So the "sad" Venusian acts "happy" and the "intelligent" Martian acts "stupid" because they don't want people to know how they really are – usually they conceive of their actual state as "bad" and don't want others to find out.

If things were not complicated enough, now we have to figure out who is really like what, and what a person's real personality is like.

The failure to understand personality, in general, accounts for more misunderstanding between men and women then the failure to understand the opposite sex. And the failure to understand personality accounts observably for most of the relationship problems, incompatibilities, lack of create, and failures that I see amongst couples.

Oddly enough when it comes to understanding the opposite sex, we all might be a little smarter than we thought. But when it comes to understanding personality…well now …..HELLLLLLPPPPPPPPPP!!!!!!!

Shortcut Personality Theory – "Feet Angles" and Personality Types

What have feet to do with personality theory and relationships?

Well I am sure there are people who can read every aspect of your feet. Just like palm readers do. I will not even go into whether or not those are exact sciences or even true.

I have never even really looked into it.

However, when it comes to relationships, one of the biggest problems is matching people of similar or compatible personality types.

As you may know, if you have been following me so far, I am a keen observer of things. Particularly things to do with meeting women, picking up women, and relating to women.

I talk about different personality types that I named the "love girls," "beautiful teases," and "gradient girls" in Chapter 2 (c).

Of course, I made these observations many years ago although they are still valid today.

These days I use more sophisticated personality observation systems. Systems that help me tremendously in my everyday life dealing with family, friends, and business associates as well as my love interests and potential love interest.

But when writing for you guys there is still some value in referring to these old barroom types, because they are easily observable and most guys have bumped into them in a bar or club once or twice or more.

Most of what I observe, both then and now, has to do with motion and emotion and the actual products people produce.

Now, I'm not here to teach you about personality theory. And in fact I won't.

As a subject, it is 100 times more complex than meeting, dating and relating to women. And there are others who have already documented workable personality technologies.

But the problem with most dating gurus is related to this personality topic. There are different types of men and different types of women. Different types of people relate differently. If you want to be successful in your dating, strategies it is not something you can ignore.

Most dating gurus do ignore personality types, however. They lump all men or all women into one category and talk about what women think or what men feel, when the truth is the variation between personality types is much greater than the variation between the sexes.

In simple words, the reason you don't feel like you understand women (or men if you are a woman) has more to do with not understanding different personality types than it has to do with the differences between the sexes.

When you ignore personality types, "pick up," meeting," and "relating" advice becomes a low percentage game - strategies that work only 1 out of 10 times on the general population. (Even though they might work a higher percentage of times in a specific situation where you have an accumulation of a certain personality type - like bars and clubs.)

Observational strategies that take personality type into consideration work 8 or 9 times out of ten on the general population - in every situation. Quite a difference in the success rate. When you master personality types and situational dating and relating methods, you become a master of this area. When you can get 8 or 9 out of 10 women that you target, you feel good and confident about yourself.

So, as I see it, the problem comes down to this. Even if you are not a master of personality types, if you had a way to meet women who were compatible with your own personality type everything would flow pretty easy. You would pretty much know what to do, know what to say, etc. It would be natural.

The problem is the majority of guys don't look at personality first they look at bodies.

And when they do look at personality they get confused. They have no systematic way of observing, understanding, and predicting human behavior. So often it takes up to six months after you meet a person to get through their "façade" or "social" personality before they start showing you who they really are, and other times it is not even six months. It is a major event that occurs - moving in together, marriage, etc. - before they let down their guard and show you who they really are.

The reason I became successful picking up women in bars and clubs 30 years ago, was I was able to spot personality types from certain patterns of motion that they exhibited. From that, I was able to predict their behavior and apply situational strategies that led them straight into my arms.

Now what I am really trying to do with all my writings is teach you guys how to observe these things for yourself. That is what will make you a master of this area. Sometimes I can give you guys my observations which can act as short cuts to leaning, and I do when I can.

So here is one of those...

This is a shortcut to personality typing and spotting that you can learn and start applying in only a few minutes from now.

It is a way you can look at a woman's body (what you do naturally) and determine a personality type in as little as a few seconds and know with a high degree of probability whether she is the right personality type for you or not.

But first a little history...
About two years ago, I was visiting my chiropractor. I had an injury to one of my legs, which kind of turned one of my feet outward. My natural feet angles where pretty much straight on - what I call 12 noon. If you were to look at a clock both my feet would be pointing to 12 noon on the clock dial. By definition, there was no angle between my feet. They were parallel when I walked.

Because of my injury to my left leg, however, my left foot was pointing to about “6 minutes to 12 on a clock face” and my right foot was pointing at 12 noon when I walked.

I asked my chiropractor about this and made a comment that assumed that most people must walk with their feet pointing to 12 noon. He said that they didn't and then he said something VERY, VERY INTERESTING. He said that the angle of the feet was controlled by a muscle and organ than had something to do with the emotion of “fear”.

Now this interested me to no end, as the emotion of fear is something that I had observed and definitely played a role in personality types and typing.

I had a little more discussion with him, but in the end, I left his office with a hypothesis to test. - That the relative angle between the feet is a measure of the emotion of fear within a person.

Now, “fear” is a very important emotion when it comes to personality typing. No “fear” makes a man very brave. A little “fear” makes him conservative, a lot of “fear” makes him afraid and even more “fear” and he is terrified. If an angry man has “fear” mixed in with his anger he becomes “covert” (backstabbing - as he is afraid to attack you from the front) rather than “overt” (face-to-face) in his anger.

Interesting this thing called "fear."

For example, my "love girls" of the barroom days had "no fear." In fact, they were so brave they scared men.

The "beautiful teases," were very afraid, they acted brave (apparent flirt) but then ran away at the first sign of real interest.

Those "gradient girls," they just had a little fear - afraid men in bars were all just a bunch of jerks.

The strategies that I evolved to pick up these different types of women were pretty much molded to handle their different types or levels of relative "fear."
Interesting....

After my talk with the chiropractor, I went back to the clubs and looked at a few examples of these "barroom" personality types with respect to this angle between the feet.

First, let me give you a few definitions in case you don't know what degrees and angles and other geometric terms are.

Let us use the face of a clock for an example. Look at the big hand and the little hand. They both start at the same point in the center of the dial, but the tips of the big hand and little hand point to different places. The two lines formed by the big hand and the little hand create an angle. The angle between them is measured geometrically in degrees.

A circle has 360 degrees. So in the clock example every minute would be a change of 6 degrees. So if we use 12 noon or 12 o'clock. The two hands are parallel and there is no angle, or 0 degrees.

When it is 12:05 pm, the hands create what is called a 30 degree angle. When it is 12:10, the two hands create a 60 degree angle. At 12:15, the two hands create a 90 degree angle and at 12:20, the two hands create a 120 degree angle.

Now the angles between human feet don't get much wider than that. (Though I have seen a few 12:22s) So for our purposes let's stop the geometry lesson here.

For our purposes though, I usually don't refer to the angles between the feet as 12:15 etc. as one has to turn one's head to see the angle correctly. If I am using the clock analogy, I usually refer to the feet positions as - left foot from 1 to 10 minutes before 12 noon or 12 noon if straight -- and the right foot from 1 to 10 minutes after noon or 12 noon if straight -- (i.e. left foot 5 minutes before noon, right foot five minutes after noon.).

Let's continue

Now "Love Girls" tended to have perfectly straight feet (both feet pointed at 12 noon). Gradient girls typically have an angle between the feet of about 12 to 24 degrees - left foot (1 or 2 minutes before noon) right foot (1 or 2 minutes after noon).

The beautiful teases typically had a angle of between 72 to 120 degrees between their feet - left foot (6 -10 minutes before noon) right foot (6-10 minutes after noon.)

Now when I say usually or tended I mean about 8 or 9 times out of ten. Or a correlation of 80-90 percent with the personality type. Now for those of you who know anything about correlation that is pretty high. That means you could make predictions about personality types and be right 8 or 9 times out of ten.

Interesting...

Does that mean everyone with straight feet are "love girls"? No. It doesn't. No more than if I said college professors all tend to have a high IQ, would it mean that everyone with a high IQ was a college professor. Love Girls are just a small subset of people with straight feet.

What it means is that people with straight feet have little or no fear. Thus, you will find them doing all kinds of things that exhibit little fear. - They might be the kind of people that start their own business, or work on commission, or take other job or career risks that others might be too afraid to do. They might be the kind of people that will talk to anyone, share their real thoughts and opinions easily, and say all kinds of personal things that others would be afraid to say out of embarrassment.

It could mean however, that if a girl with straight feet ever gets herself in a position where she is terribly horny, without a boyfriend, and the only thing she can think of is going to a bar with the intention of picking up some guy to get laid, well then she would most likely go about it like a "Love Girl" and NOT like a "Beautiful tease" or "Gradient Girl".

But be careful how you interpret these things or it could get you in trouble.

Remember, feet angles give you the relative amount of fear. That is all we know for sure. Everything else is a correlation.

So let's talk about fear for a second. There is situationally appropriate fear and generalized fear. Everyone - all personality types - should have situationally appropriate fear. So we all might feel some fear walking down some bad street with gangsters and hoodlums all around us late at night. We all might feel some fear trusting our life to some doctor performing an operation where only 50% of the people survive.

It is generalized fear - non situationally appropriate fear - that tells us more about personality type. Being shy and afraid to talk to women is a form of fear. Being afraid to talk to a bunch of people in front of a public speaking class is a form of fear. Being afraid to invest one's money in a business venture is a form of fear.

Being afraid to leave one's nine to five job security to start your own business is a form of fear. Being afraid of the dark is a form of fear. Being afraid of the unknown is a form of fear. Being afraid of what your friends might think about something you say or do is a form of fear. Being afraid of looking ridiculous in front of your friends is a form of fear.

These generalized-fears and non-situationally appropriate fears determine personality type.

You see the "Love Girl" is confident and fearless. She isn't afraid of men, so when she wants to get laid she walks into a bar knowing she's sexy and knowing she can intimidate men. She just looks every man in the eye because she wants a confident fearless man - just like her.

The gradient girl is not as confident and fearless. She is afraid that most of the guys in bars are jerks. So she approaches the situation with that bias. She is not so afraid that she will run away from men who will approach her, but she will banter with them and just say "no" when it comes to the real "pick up" moment because her fear biases her towards the viewpoint that men in this situation should be feared.

The "beautiful tease" is deathly afraid of men. She is in the bar because she is trying to overcome her fears. She is beautiful and has learned that men will respond to her, so she flirts to get attention and attraction which make her feel good. But as soon as some guy gets really interested, she runs away. She is deathly afraid and can't confront it. It takes a guy who understand this and make her feel totally safe and in control to seduce her. Such was the technique that I worked out 30 years ago.

So how do we use this "angle of the feet" observation to help you guys with your dating and relating problems.

Well there is one giant maxim that I am going to give you in a moment, but first let me say the way you use this is to make observations for yourself. I'm not here to give you lessons in personality theory. Just know that there are different personality types that correlate with the "angles between the feet."

Start by observing the angle of your own feet. Then observe the feet of the people that you know and observe similarities and differences in personality. Start out with major differences, like people with straight feet versus people with very wide feet. See which angles you get along with best.

There is no right or wrong here, or good or bad. There is just compatibility.

So HERE is the GIANT MAXIM. (a truth or basic principle).

MAXIM:1 - You should not get into a relationship with anyone who is more than 2-3 minutes on a clock face or 12- 24 degrees (geometrically) different than your own "angle between the feet." People who are more than 2-3 minutes or 12-24 degrees different from you are going to have personality types that are too different from you to achieve total compatibility with them.

Remember, however, that this is only true 80-90% of the time. There will be exceptions to the rule. WHY? Because people have "façade" or "social" feet angles just like, they have "façade" or "social personalities."

For example, people who are in the acting or modeling industry may be trained to walk with their feet very straight. (12 noon). So you may have a "beautiful tease" that has straight feet because she was trained to walk that way not because she has "no fear!" Get it.

People have accidents to their legs and feet and back, etc. that can change the angle between their feet and give you a false interpretation. Usually, however, it is one foot that is out - not both, but I have met people with both out as results of accidents.

MAXIM 2: - If you are in a relationship with someone who has an angle between their feet more than 2-3 minutes on a clock face or 12- 24 degrees (geometrically) different than your own "angle between the feet," and if you get along beautifully, than forget about it. You are probably in that area of the 10-20% exceptions that don't correlate. Ultimately, you have to observe the person in front of you and not their feet.

However, if you are having trouble with this person in a relationship, then observe their exact angle and make a point of meeting other people with that angle and talking to them. Talk to your guy friends with a similar angle. There is a personality type here, get to know and understand it. They are different from you. They don't think like you do. So throw all you assumptions out the window and get to know the personality type in front of you.

If you can do that then you will be able to improve the understanding between each other in the relationship. The closer they are in relation to your own "angle between the feet" however, the better chance you have for long-term survival of your relationship.

WHY DID I GIVE YOU THIS DATA?

This is one of those observations that took me years to observe and figure out. You can benefit from it immediately.

Stick with girls (and guy friends) with similar foot angle and you will find you get along better with them.

Does this mean that we shouldn't have friends with different foot angles? NO! It doesn't. It just means for those real close relationships that you can choose - girlfriend, boss, best friend, etc. - you would get along better and stand a better chance of achieving a long term successful relationship with someone who is within 2-3 minutes of your own foot angle.

Remember also, there are different kinds of relationships. Some friend or girlfriend you see once a week doesn't have to be as compatible with you as someone you live with or work with every day. Use this data to qualify those kinds of situations.

Make some observations of your own. Look at your own feet angle. Look at the people that you get along with best. What is their foot angle? Look at the people that you definitely do not like. What is their foot angle? You will discover trends. You might notice that 6 out of 10 people that you really like have a foot angle within 2-3 minutes of yours and that 3 out of 10 people that you do not like at all have a foot angle within 5-10 minutes from yours.

However, foot angle is immediately noticeable. It gives you a quick 80-90% reliable method of sizing up people fast. It also lets you see through facades and "social" personalities as most people do not pay attention to feet and do not try to fake the angle of their feet.

Once you start making observations you can associate with the various foot angles you will be able to predict people with relative accuracy (80-90% right).

Now as a final note, I want to say, “Please don't believe me. Do not assume what I am telling you is true. Go observe for yourself."

Look at all of your friends and relatives. Correlate the angles with their personality types. Go to a busy street corner or a mall and start observing these foot angles. A simple test or computation is the percent of perfectly straight feet (both pointing to 12 noon). Count the number of people with straight feet out of every 10 that walk by or every 100.

Do it by sexes. Do it by age groups. Do it by races. You will see some interesting things.

Here are some of my observations after 1000s of observations.

In Los Angeles/Beverly Hills where I made most of my observations, on the average:

1-2 to men out of 10 have straight feet.
2-4 women out of 10 have straight feet.
8-9 out of 10 children under 8-10 have straight feet.

The above was the same for black, white, and brown Americans but oddly
5 out of 10 Chinese Americans have straight feet. (didn't look at sex differences)

In Japan (Tokyo)

7- 8 out of 10 women have straight feet
1-2 out of 10 men have straight feet.

Walking or standing may be different for different people. Walking is a better determination, but how one stands can also be a clue to hidden tendencies if it is greatly different.

I am still accumulating data in this area. If you make any interesting observations about any of this please tell me about them at ---one of my various blogs or forums at www.DatingToRelating.com , www.DatingToRelating.net , or www.MeYouWorld.net

4) THE BASIC SOLUTION – OBSERVATION – HOW TO DEVELOP STRATEGIES

Perception Channels

So in a previous Chapter we discussed how women are more perceptive than men in relationships. They see more things than we see. However, this does not mean that this is necessarily a physical ability. Perhaps it is just a learned ability, and perhaps men can become, for most practical purposes, just as perceptive as women.

Consequently, in the last Chapter discussing this I gave you some basic ways to increase your perception. Here are some more.

One of the best ways for men to increase their perception of what is going on with women is to look at (perceive) different channels of communication.

There are many, many channels that a communication can be delivered across and perceived, but let's just take up four major ones here.

1) Physical communications
2) Verbal communications
3) Mental communications
4) Emotional communications

1) Physical - a woman smiles at you. She winks. She wiggles her hips as she walks. She has good posture... She has bad posture...She touches your hand. She takes your arm. She kisses you are the cheek, or on the lips... She turns her cheek when you go to kiss her. She shakes your hand when you go to kiss her. These are all physical communications. They are saying something to you. You need to perceive them and understand them.

The two most important things to perceive about physical communications are who originated what, and in what direction is the physical closeness going.

Origination - It means one thing if she leans into you and gives you a kiss. It can mean another thing if you lean into her and she lets you kiss her.

If she originates something, that means she is definitely interested in it. If you originate it she may just allow you to do it as she is being polite or not wanting to embarrass you.
The classic case is regarding phone numbers. If the girl offers you her phone number without asking, you pretty much know she wants you to call and will accept and/or return your call.

If you ask her for her phone number, she might just give it to you to be polite and not to embarrass you. Or maybe she is just trying to get rid of you.

Probably one of the most frequent questions I get on our website is "How do I get the girl to call me back?" Girls are adept at getting rid of obtrusive guys. That number may just be voice mail, or it may be she won't answer numbers she doesn't know.

Motion toward/Motion away - If you give a girl a compliment and she leans back or steps back away from you, that means one thing. If she leans into you or steps in towards you after a compliment, that means another thing.

Motion towards you means interest. Motion away from you means lack of interest. So when the girl moves towards you, touches you, and thanks you for the compliment - that is good. Continue. It is working. When she moves away from you after the compliment - even if she says thank you with a nice smile - that is bad. Time to regroup. Do not do that again.

(Motion toward can also be mental, emotional, or verbal. So if you give her a compliment and she gets a little happier, or she talks to you a little more - that is good too!)

2) Verbal - The verbal communication we are interested in are communications having to do with "sexual attraction" etc. This is a gradient area. At its lowest form there is no sex talk and no response to sex talk. The first gradient of interest is "negative sex talk." It is important to perceive what a person originates to you here. A girl who is really not interested in you, won't bring up sex as a topic and won't respond (contribute to it) when you bring it up.

A girl who is interested in you will often begin originating sexual interest to you by "negative sex talk." (Statements like: "Guys are jerks. They only want sex." "Don't expect sex with me." Etc.) Do not be put off by this. Understand it for what it is. (If she originates negative sex talk to you, she is interested in you. It is different if you originate sex talk and she responds negatively. That is a different condition.) If a girl originates negative sex talk to you, respond in like kind. Do not argue with her. Agree. That will make her feel safe and then she will move up to "positive sex talk."

If a girl originates positive sex talk, it should be clear what to do. Respond in like kind. (If you are interested in her.)

It does not matter here if the girl is saying negative things about you are someone else. Match the negative or positive element and then match what she is saying about you or others.

3) Mental communications are all that stuff about what you like and what you do not like and your interests and hobbies, etc. Now the thing here is that most guys do the "Motion toward" and "Motion away" thing here innately. They will say they like "hiking" just because they know the girl likes hiking. They will pretend to be a gentleman because they know the girl likes that.

The problem is if you are looking for a real relationship, this is the one area where you don't want to do whatever works. If you want to have a good relationship then it starts with being honest and true to yourself. There are plenty of girls out there. Find one who thinks like you do and likes the things you do. Do not compromise your integrity and say you like things you do not just to get a girl.

Talk to the girl. Tell her honestly what your likes and dislikes and attitudes about things are. Find out what her likes, dislikes, and attitudes are. It is important here that you really perceive what you are getting yourself into.

If you hook up with someone you have very little in common with, chances are you won't have a good relationship.

4) Emotional communication - This is a good one to perceive. Is she a happy person, a sad person, an angry person? Are you both on the same emotional wavelength? This one is sort of like the mental communication. Do not pretend to be something you are not. If you pretend to be happy and you aren't, then the person you hook up with won't like you anymore when they find out you are really a sad person. It is better to find someone who is ok with sad people to begin with.

Now here is another mistake. Many people - both men and women - try to hook up with people they know they are not compatible with for one reason or another. They feel like they can "change" them over time and then they will get along better. The problem is it does not work 90% of the time. So do not bother. If you innately know someone is wrong for you - drop them - split up. There are plenty of fish in the sea. Do not try to change people. It rarely works and it usually makes someone very miserable before the invariable break up.

These are four communication channels that you can start looking at to better understand women (and people in general). However, there is one more major concept you need to get. And this is the relative "complexity" of the total communication.

Here is where it usually gets interesting. You see all this might be pretty easy to perceive and grasp if everyone just gave us simple communications. You know, the girl says, "I like you" and gives you a warm affectionate hug and kiss.

But what does it mean, and what do you do when:

1) The girl gives you her phone number but won't return your call.
2) The girl smiles at you in the club, but shoots you down when you ask her to dance.
3) The girl goes out on four dates with you, but won't even give you a kiss.
4) You have a pleasant date and conversation, but she gives you no clue that she is even vaguely interested in you in any way more than friends.

These are all complex communications. They involve more than one channel of communication and the channels unfortunately send mixed inconsistent messages.

Now guys have different ways of dealing with complex messages. Some guys pull out the good message and ignore the bad message. Other guys ignore the good message and pay attention to only the bad message.

There are three simple rules here.

a) Pay attention to the whole communication delivered across all communication channels. That is the clue to understanding.
b) Simple communications require simple answers.
c) Complex communications require complex answers.

Let's go back to my favorite examples the barroom types that I have been referring to: "Love Girls," "Gradient Girls" and "Beautiful teases."

These personality types are good examples of simple communications through complex communications.

The "Love Girls" were giving a simple consistent message delivered across several channels. They dressed sexy. They walked sexy. They looked every guy in the eye looking for a response. - Everything about them said, "I'm hot and ready" - no inconsistencies.

The mistake I saw guys make with "Love Girls" over and over again, was that the majority of guys couldn't confront the simplicity of a beautiful hot and ready girl. All the guys I watched (except for a few now and then) needed time to figure out what to do. They would go talk to their buddies and gulp down a few beers.

Problem was, by that time the Love Girl was either gone or taken. These girls were simple. All you had to do was walk up to them and ask them to dance. No games. You danced sexy. You got close. Then you asked them to go to your place and they did.

Now the ultra complex girls were the "Beautiful Teases."

The "Beautiful Tease" would smile, flirt, and even say nice things to you to get your attention. However, when you went chasing after her, she would shoot you down, ignore you, or pay attention to some other guy. Then when you thought it was hopeless she would smile and talk to you again and get you all revved up again.

The Beautiful Tease confused most guys. They don't know what's going on. She likes me. She doesn't like me. She likes me...after a while most guys just think she is weird or a bitch and then just walk away….until she smiles and flirts with them again.

You can't just walk up to a Beautiful Tease and say "Would you like to dance." It won't work. She requires a complex answer to her complex communication. Her complex communication was: I'm scared of men, but I'm trying to get over it. So I'm testing the water I'm trying to approach men, but I really need a guy who won't scare me.

Hence my strategy of standing next to her and ignoring her, and talking about how hot some other girl is.

The regular "gradient girls" are complex too, but not quite as complex as the Beautiful Teases. Their communication is "Guys in bars are jerks, but I'm lonely and really want to meet someone so I'm here anyway. So you can't be direct as you are with the Love Girl, even if you get what they are saying. You can't simply say "I'm not a jerk." That won't be received well by her. You have to be equally complex.

Hence the rant and rave about how everyone is messed up and phony in the bar, and look at that guy - what a jerk, etc.

If you deliver your communication sufficiently complex, she'll believe you, and believe you are not a jerk.

Communications have motion patterns to them. if you want to increase your perception watch the motion pattern associated with a multiple channel communication.

Use your eyes. Watch people. Look at the physical, verbal, emotional, and mental communications. Then and only them do you pay attention to the content. The content of the communication is the least valuable. This is how people usually lie and try to deceive you and themselves.

An example of content being worthless involves my first wife. I met her at college. She saw me giving a speech and got a crush on me. She was a freshman. I was a junior. We started dating and then she revealed she had to break up with me because she had a boyfriend back home. She would go see him every weekend.

Did I pay any attention to the content? NO!

I looked at the whole communication - physically, emotionally and mentally she was continually moving closer to me. She liked me. She saw me 5 days a week. She saw him two. If she were really in love with him, she wouldn't even be talking to me.

My response whenever she told me she couldn't see me anymore was to ignore the content and look at the other channels. I simply said "Ok, how about one last meal together." And we would have that meal and spend the rest of the day together. I did that every day for about two weeks and she broke up with me every day for two weeks, until one day she finally told me she broke up with him. The rest is history.

Motion Toward – Motion Away

Many of the suggestions in this book are evolved techniques. Techniques (strategies) that evolved from theory into an application with specific steps that you can apply without ever understanding the theory that the technique evolved from.

In this section, I am going to give you the theory and basic technique which if you understand and apply allows you to manufacture the other techniques in this book and many more. It allows you to be situationally totally correct 100% of the time. You will never be guessing at what to do if you apply the basic technique outlined and described in this chapter.

Can any guy do it? Well any guy could do it. It does not require a high IQ or anything, but it does require an attitude. You must have the attitude that you are willing to look, listen, and learn. (Let us call them the THREE Ls)

If you have the kind of personality or attitude that is not compatible with looking, listening and learning, this will only work for you to the degree that you are compatible with the THREE Ls.

I have also met guys who state that they want to look, listen and learn, but even when given precise instruction they are terrible at it. They could look at the exact same thing that I am looking at but not see the obvious thing that I see.

Fortunately, I have discovered why these guys can't see what I see and I have learned how to train them and I will go over that in this Chapter. Briefly, what I look at is the total motion and direction of motion (toward, away, parallel, etc.) contained within a situation. People who look at what I am looking at and don't see what I see either are not looking at the total Motion contained in a situation or they are looking at it but putting greater importance on some other variable that they see than motion.

For example, we have many channels of communication which all contain motion. Some of the more obvious channels are:

Verbal
Physical
Emotional
Mental
Sexual

Each of these channels can have a different motion going on at the same time. – When a girl says she likes you, and leans in and kisses you – the motion on all five channels is consistent. It is easy to interpret.

However, when you are at a party and some new girl you have never met before says "Not so fast, Charlie." as she leans into you, rubs up against you and whispers sexily in your ear. And continues with "I have a boyfriend." Then splits five minutes later never to be seen the rest of the night even though she said, "I'll be back. Don't go anywhere."

What is going on here?

Well I have seen guys look at ONLY the motion contained in one channel of such a complicated communication. They will only pay attention to the fact that she rubbed up against them (sexual motion toward) and align everything else with that motion. They will convince themselves that the girl really likes them and is going to be dumping her boyfriend for them.

What they fail to see is although there was a sexual motion toward (rubbing up against them); there was also a verbal motion away (I have a boyfriend) and a physical motion away (she never came back.)

If every girl you ever approached responded with "You know I like you" and gave you a kiss, or said, "I don't like you" and walked away. Life would be simple.

But unfortunately life isn't like that. A lot of the girls you approach (because you have failed to observe their motion before you approached them), are already turned off by you on one motion channel or another (like sexual or non-verbal). Before you even opened your mouth they have developed a bias against you, and are responding to your approach with mixed motion. (They are attracted to you on one channel and turned off on another.)

Overall total MOTION is the key observation. And that breaks down into CHANNELS of communication and MOTION TOWARDS and MOTION AWAY. (And to a lesser extent you will have NO MOTION and PARALLEL MOTION.)

Now if you are with me so far, there is hope for you.

SO let's move on to the next important principal you must know and make. -- There are different personality types. Different personality types have different motion patterns in general, and different motion patterns in different situations.

So you see until you have a lot of observational experience in a lot of situations with a lot of different personality types, you will have to rely on strategies. Strategies yield low results over all, as strategies are only meant to handle specific personality types in specific situations.

Any of the strategies I have given you in this book or my website or that other dating gurus give you all work. But they only work in certain situations with certain personality types; hence they work a small percentage of time if you employed the strategy universally. Worse yet, if the strategy only works on a personality type that you don't like, you will only get girls with it that ultimately you are not attracted to. You might get laid but you won't get a long-term relationship out of it.

Now the observational technique I am teaching you here gets around all that. It gives you basic principles to create attraction with ANY personality type. You would be smart to find one that is compatible with your own personality. An easy way to do that was explained in a previous discussion about personality and "feet angles."

Now let us get into the specifics of how to observe motion.

i) Purposes in Observing Motion

First, let us look at our purposes in observing motion. Our purposes in observing motion are twofold:

1) To determine what the exact attraction pattern of a target personality or situational type is; and
2) To determine what to do (how to approach, how to respond) in exact situations.

Let us take (1) first.

Say you have a personality type – like friendly outgoing girls, or sarcastic girls, or intelligent career minded girls – or a situational type – like hot girls in clubs, or girls at church, or girls who work in mall stores. We can observe these kinds of girls over time and see some different motion patterns and perhaps some sub-types emerge. If you read Chapter 2 (c) and my examples of how to pick up girls in bar and clubs, you will see how I applied this observational technique to classify club types and develop a motion strategy for each one. The result – I got laid every night I went to clubs for months and months on end until I got tired of doing it. My success rate with targets was about 90%.

Where do you observe? - Pick out anywhere you would like to go to meet the kind of women you would like to meet: a mall, a library, church, a bar, whatever.

Make a program to go there at least once a week and practice looking and observing.

What do you observe? – Observe the target woman's interaction with men. If you can observe how she deals with other men first that is best, but if you can't, you will have to approach her and observe her reactions to you. Start out with anything. It doesn't matter. Find a strategy in this book or any other book and try using it.

What you want is a lot of situational observations until you see a pattern emerge. I got the "beautiful tease" pattern and the "love girl" pattern by simply watching "beautiful teases" and "love girls" interact with other men. Once I spotted the pattern, I approached them with my handle and it was instant success. So the point is sometimes you can totally get the pattern by watching women interact with other men.

"Gradient girls" however was not something you could observe by watching these women with other men. First of all, "gradient girls" aren't as dramatic as other women and the interactions that lead to success are much longer in terms of time. Thus observing other people did not help me in seeing this pattern. I saw this pattern by approaching these women applying the techniques and theory I am going to give you below. Getting rejected a number of times (but learning all the while). And finally seeing a pattern emerge which I then applied a handle to. From that point forward, there was 90% success.

Now we move into our second purpose – to determine what to do (how to approach, how to respond) in exact situations.

Opening strategy. When approaching any woman in any situation – first let me address one thing. I am going to assume you are approaching "hot" women in this discussion. If you are approaching "normal" or "ugly" women all of this gets easier to the degree you are approaching "ugly". That is as long as the "ugly" or "normal" woman is sane.

"Ugly" women are like men. They don't get approached very often. Like most men, "ugly" women will not be rude or blow off someone who approaches them with a sincere attraction or interest or compliment. To the degree, you know that the woman you are approaching does not get approached a lot, you can practically say anything you want on approach as long as it is sincere and not rude. They will rarely turn you down. (Unless they have a personality disorder or a personality type that is totally incompatible with your own - and there are a few normal and ugly women who will still react as if they are "hot.")

"Hot" women on the other hand get hit up upon sometimes once a day, five times a day, twenty times a day, etc. depending on the environment they live and work in. They have learned the hard way that most guys are just interested in them for sex. They have learned to blow guys off either overtly ("get out of here creep") or covertly (they give you their voicemail number and never return the call) and have become quite expert at it. They can get sex anytime they want it, and their attention is NOT on that factor. They – like most humans – want to be appreciated for who they are inside. Not what they are on the outside.

So back to our point.

Opening strategy for "hot" women. When approaching any "hot" woman in any situation, remember you may be the twentieth guy today to approach them, the one hundred and fortieth guy this week, the six hundredth guy this month and the seven thousand three hundredth guy this year to approach them. Keep that in mind because the first basic principle you want to apply is to be different from all those other guys.

If you want to get her attention and begin to create some attraction you must be different. Remember what I told you when discussing picking up girls in bars and clubs? Be "Interesting and Unique."

You see the guy who has the balls to walk up to and confront the horny "Love Girl" is interesting and unique to her because most guys are too scared to do it. He only has to open his mouth and confidently ask her to dance. The guy who tells the "Tease Girl" she's not that hot, but has a good personality is "interesting and Unique" to her, because ALL guys reach at these girls and tell them how beautiful they are. The guy who can dish out negative sex talk to a "Regular Girl" is interesting and Unique" to her because she never finds guys like this in the club. And of course the Boredom Girls, who get guy after guy after guy hitting on them and kissing their ass find "Cocky and Funny" totally interesting and Unique. Boredom girls are a kind of random, casual, and pointless-talk band of girl, and Cocky and Funny is random and pointless talk.

SO whatever you do when approaching a girl for the first time in any situation is try to be "Interesting and Unique."

Now if you remember what I told you about "feet angles", limit your approach to women within 2-3 minutes of your own feet angles and you will have a better chance for a natural interest. But if you want to learn about different personality types and what works then approach any woman with any "angle" but note what her "feet angle" is. Because you are going to observe that there will be different strategy that works for women that have different "feet angles".

The best opening line is simply "Hi" or to make a comment about something that she already has her attention on.

Now from this point forward you are going to try to observe every motion she makes on every communication channel you can observe and make a mental note of it. When you are done with the interaction, I would even have a notebook handy and write down my observations about the interaction.

Look at and note the SEXUAL MOTION (in terms of MOTION TOWARD you and MOTION AWAY from you) on the following basic channels as you interact:

PHYSICAL – is she showing any sexual interest (motion toward you) with her eyes, a smile of delight, a slight touch? Or is she moving away by being reserved in manner and tone, looking away from you and not at you on purpose as if disinterested, stepping back from you if you get too close.

VERBAL – does she keep the conversation going (motion toward) once you open it, or are you doing all the work? Does she verbally flirt with you or give you compliments. Or is she refusing to flirt, telling you she has a boyfriend in response to your flirt?

MENTAL – is she moving toward you mentally by saying things that you agree with or know a lot about, or have a common interest in, or is she moving away from you by mentioning all sorts of things you disagree with, have no interest in, would never want to do, etc.

If she is moving toward you mentally, you will become engrossed in conversation rather easily with no effort. There will be plenty of things to talk about with no effort. The conversation will go on much longer than you planned. If she is moving away from you mentally there will be nothing to talk about, short sentences, short responses, it will be like pulling teeth to maintain a conversation.

EMOTIONAL – is she moving toward you (express and share similar emotions to your own) or away from you (express emotions much different from your usual set.) You have to be able to observe yourself to do this one correctly. You may be attracted to say bright cheerful women, but you may be a resentful, angry man. If that is the case, guess what? It is not going to work. (Not unless you sincerely want to change your own attitude. And if that is the case, better to do that first before getting involved with anyone.)

Remember that "feet angles" correspond with this emotional vector about 80%. So a shortcut to the emotional observation is similar "feet angle."

SEXUAL – is she moving toward you (moving up the scale of sexual interest towards intercourse? Or is she moving away from you (down the scale of sexual interest) or not moving at all (stays at one level doesn't move)? The key here is to recognize that "Negative Sex Talk" is the first level of sexual interest. When a woman brings up sex by talking negative about sex, – (you can't have sex with me, all guys just want sex, I don't like sex, etc.) – it is the first level of sexual interest.

ii) Scale of Sexual Motion

- Negative Sex talk – Talks about not having or not liking sex or aspects of sex
- Positive Sex talk – Talks about liking, enjoying, wanting sex or aspects of it.
- No touch (just verbal communications)
- No touch but visual channels –eye contact, smiles, Be There interest
- Conservative formal touch – Kiss, touch, shake hands, hugs
- Repeated accidental touch
- Little touches, finger taps, etc
- Getting real close – to turn on excite
- Little touches to turn on – knees, thigh, hair, etc.
- Nudity or other visual turn on, to turn on.
- Kissing
- Making Out
- Light petting
- Heavy Petting
- Intercourse

iii) Adjusting as You Interact. – This is the crux of learning what to do.

You can adjust while talking to one individual or you can adjust from one individual to another as you learn about a type.

EXAMPLE 1– A woman is shopping in the grocery store. You position yourself next to her. First, you have made these observations. She is moderately hot, has very good statuesque posture. She seems to be very intently looking at a can of beans. You notice she has no ring on her finger. She seems to be alone, and her feet are pointing left foot 11 o'clock right foot 1 o'clock.

You turn looking directly at her and say with a smile and pleasant tone "Excuse me, but is that a good brand of beans."

She doesn't look up, but continues looking at the beans and replies "It's okay." She continues to look at the beans and not you, and makes no further comment.

[So I mentally note. NO MOTION TOWARD which sometimes equates to the same thing as MOTION AWAY. Physically she didn't look at me. Verbally she did not try to keep a conversation going. And emotionally and mentally there was no connection at all. No motion toward.

So the first thing I note is that a direct friendly approach did not work with this person and this personality type – which I don't know what it is yet other than "left foot 11 o'clock right foot 1 o'clock."

So, if I want to continue with her, I need to correct immediately in a direction that is more likely to elicit a "motion toward" from her. I also want to broaden my observations, as even though she has no ring on her finger, there may be boyfriend around the corner or nearby, which could account for her behavior. For example, even if I gave up at this point. I might still want to watch her for a while for research reasons to see if she does have a boyfriend in the store or not. If she does, then I have a "Type" and a research project – How to approach a girl in a store who has a boyfriend nearby and get her phone number.

But if I wanted to immediately correct my approach and try to salvage her – say she is really, really hot- then what I know at this time is I need to change my direct friendly approach.]

So I turn away from her (rather than looking and talking to her) I make a pointed sigh as I look at a can of beans and say, "This sucks, I have no idea." Kind of laughing to myself out loud.

[Now this is pretty much "trial and error" at this point, but there is nothing wrong with that. Most guys do the same old dumb thing which never works over and over and over again for 20 years or so before they try something different. When you get no response to your physical-verbal-mental-emotional approach to a woman, start changing the variables instantly. You can make one or two mistakes and still recover. It is when you make five or ten mistakes in a row that you will have a hard time recovering.

So what I did here is change my physical approach from direct to indirect – I turn from looking and talking directly to her and imitate what she is doing. I use an indirect motion. I look at the beans and talk indirectly to her almost as if I am talking to myself. I also change my pleasant friendly emotion (smile and pleasant tone) to one of slight irritation – "This sucks." Now I am going to wait and observe her reaction to my new indirect MOTION toward her.]

Surprisingly, she responds with a sarcastic "That's life" - still looking at her beans. Then she quickly adds, "If you can't cook you should probably get the Lucky Brand. They taste fairly good and they are hard to mess up."

"Really?" I say sort of questioningly amazed still looking at the beans not her. [I got a MOTION TOWARDS from her by this approach so I am not going to blow it now by doing something else. I will hold this position until I get more motion towards from her – for example, she turns to me or glances at me, etc. At that time, I will imitate whatever she does again.]

"Yeah" she says. "They are over there on your left." She points and while pointing she turns her head slightly and glances at me for the first time.

[Now this is more MOTION TOWARDS - I got physical motion towards (she glances at me) as well as verbal (She kept the conversation going when it wasn't even clear that I was talking to her) as well as mental and emotional (she is moving toward helping me mentally and moving toward me emotionally once I changed my tone from friendly to slightly irritated.]

END OF EXAMPLE ONE – Now there are all kinds of directions I could take this girl in this make believe example. I got her moving towards me by simply adjusting and changing my physical approach and emotional approach after the opening statement and response.

This is immensely important to see, because most guys blow it with women in the first few minutes of a conversation. If a woman is MOVING AWAY from you and you don't perceive it and ADJUST, you will forever lose her as a prospect even if you somehow manage to keep a conversation going. You can make one or two mistakes in your approach or response to a woman, before you adjust. That is about it. If you continue to make mistakes, you will be "typified" by her and that will be that.

NOW you can also get off to a good start with a woman and blow it later on by not observing the motions. The process is always the same. It is something that you continually monitor. It never ends. When you are first meeting and approaching a woman you have literally to watch the multi channel motion and response to every word and sentence that you say. This is how you establish attraction.

Once you know someone you can be more casual in your observations as you will usually know what to do or say and not have to watch every word. Nevertheless, you still must watch the ebb and flow. If someone suddenly starts a MOTION AWAY from you on any or several channels, you must perceive it and correct it immediately to maintain the relationship.

NOW in EXAMPLE 1 above, if I had gotten flustered after her lack of response and didn't know what to do, it is ok to walk away from the situation, analyze it later, and approach the same or similar situation with a different approach next time. So in that case, I would have simply approached the next woman in that situation by standing next to her, not looking at her and saying aloud "This sucks, I have no idea about beans." - perhaps shaking my head and then slightly glancing over at her.

JUST OBSERVE and ADJUST if there is NO MOTION or MOTION AWAY. If you get MOTION TOWARDS you as a response, then keep doing what you did to create the motion towards and only change when the woman changes the gradient of interaction.

So in EXAMPLE 1 above, after the woman turns and points and glances at me, I can quickly glance back, but I mainly want to keep looking at the beans and talking indirectly to her. If at some point she turns totally around and starts talking directly to me, I would then perhaps turn and start directly talking to her, but all the while minutely observing if that was still working and still creating motion toward.

If she turned and started talking to me, and I turned and started talking to her, and she quickly turned away from me again, I would quickly go back to what worked and know better than to respond by turning to her the next time she turned back to me.

There are strange people in the world and you will get strange patterns evolving when you do these observations, but that is life.

For the most part, most people are like the "gradient girls" in the clubs. But "hot girls" can be all over the place and have many typical and many non-typical patterns.

Rather than relying on trial-and-error from scratch, I will give you some set patterns of motions that you can try in situations to see which ones work and which ones don't.

iv) Set Patterns of Motion

MOTION TOWARDS can also be called REACH and MOTION AWAY can be called WITHDRAW.

BEING THERE or NOT BEING THERE is also another important consideration when looking at MOTION.

BEING THERE or NOT BEING THERE determines whether or not you even have the ability to communicate to someone. And BEING THERE or NOT BEING THERE can be a MOTION TOWARDS or a MOTION AWAY in itself.

A person or friend who is always BEING THERE for you and suddenly stops BEING THERE is making a MOTION AWAY from you. Conversely, someone who had never been there for you who suddenly starts being there a lot for you is making a MOTION TOWARD.

Here are some MOTION PATTERNS

Reach
Withdraw
No Motion
Being there on a reach
Being there on a withdraw
Being there with no motion
Reaching on a withdraw
Withdrawing on a reach
Reaching and withdrawing at the same time
Reaching on some communication channels withdrawing on others.
Alternately and repeatedly reaching then withdrawing

I could even get more esoteric than above and add such patterns as reaching on a reach and reaching with no-motion and withdrawing with a withdraw, etc. but I will let you discover more complicated patterns on your own.

Let me just explain some of the above patterns and how we observe them and use them to meet, pick-up, seduce, attract, and relate to women.

Pure reach is simple. You communicate you are interested across ALL Channels.

Pure withdraw is also simple. You are gone. You are not even there any more. I often have to give advice to women to use pure withdraw when they want to end it with a man. When a woman won't see you, won't talk to you, won't answer the phone, you eventually get it. When a woman spends hours on the phone telling you how she wants to end it or keeps meeting you because she wants to be friends, etc. you still think you have a chance. Pure withdraw is simple and doesn't confuse the issue by reaching across any channel.

No Motion - is a pattern that is usually confusing when it is on the sexual/physical channel only. Ever have a female friend you get along with, but never seems to make a motion towards sexuality. And no matter what you say or do there just is no motion on that vector. What is usually going on here is that the guy needs to OBSERVE the physical and sexual channels more. Usually the guy is relying upon REACH on the other channels – verbal, emotional, mental to carry him into the sexual. You have to start observing what is going on with her specifically on the physical/sexual channel and see what creates MOTION TOWARD or MOTION AWAY or NO MOTION for her on that channel.

Find out. Learn. Use the VERBAL CHANNEL and the EMOTIONAL CHANNEL to get information out of her and to learn what creates motion toward for her. Sometimes it is a case of a guy just not creating anything physical at all. In that case, start making motion toward her on the physical channel. But if that is not the case and she doesn't respond to your physical approaches than use the verbal and emotional to find out what makes her tick.

<u>Being there on a reach</u> – This is what guys normally do. You walk up to a girl and tell her how much you like her and how hot she is, etc.

<u>Being there on a withdraw</u> – This is an indirect approach. You walk up to a girl and don't talk about how much you like her an how hot she is, etc. You find something else to talk about and come up with a good reason to continue to be there in the future as a first gradient to meeting a girl or creating a relationship without ever expressing or showing sexual interest on any channel.

When being there on a withdraw be cognizant of all your channels of communication. I have a friend who finally learned not to talk about sex VERBALLY but he still gets this gleam in his eye and a smile on his face when he is talking to a hot woman, which gives him away PHYSICALLY no matter what he says verbally.

<u>Being there with no motion</u> – sometimes there is a woman with the gleam in her eye and a smile on her face and you know she wants you. You don't have to make a motion toward or away. Just be there and sooner or later she will jump you.

Sometime the no motion on one channel is done hand in hand with motion on another channel. Sometimes any motion on the sexual channel away or toward would blow the deal for you. So you apply no motion on the sexual channel while making a motion toward on the emotional or mental channel. Eventually the motion toward on the mental or emotional channel makes an attraction and causes the other person to make a motion toward you on the sexual channel.

<u>Reaching on a withdraw</u> – For example, you want to bring up sex but you don't want to seem reachy about it. So you talk about NOT having sex. You announce to your date that you don't want to get involved with someone sexually too soon, that you want to get to know them first, etc. You brought up the topic (you have reached) but you did it in a way that the person will not react to the reach as they will see the withdraw (you don't want to jump into things too soon.)

<u>Withdrawing on a reach</u> – Calling someone up and saying, "Get out of my life. I never want to see you again." That would definitely be withdrawing on a reach.

<u>Reaching and withdrawing at the same time</u> – There are a multitude of ways this can be accomplished. Most typically, it involves <u>Reaching on some communication channels while withdrawing on others and alternately and repeatedly reaching then withdrawing.</u>

EXAMPLE 2

Let me give you an example of a complex reaching and withdrawing at the same time pattern.

The first time I began using the above terminology and observing the same is when I was a young man learning how to pick up women in bars and clubs. Every bar and club, it seems, has their own set of "Beautiful Tease" women who frequent the establishment or who in some cases work there.

In any case these women usually originate flirting with you, or they are nice and friendly to you and in one way or another give you the distinct impression they are interested in you. It gets you to the point that no matter how shy you are you are ready to act upon their flirting and friendliness.

The moment you do, however they drop you like a hot potato. Most guys don't get it because they are sure these women really like them, so they kind of get hung up on these girls and continue to hang around them hoping for some more attention. Every once-in-a -while they will give you some more attention then just drop you again.

After watching these girls for a month or so hanging out in bars and clubs I finally began to see their pattern. They would make a MOTION TOWARDS guys but as soon as the guys made a significant MOTION TOWARDS them, they would make a MOTION AWAY. Moreover, after a month or so, I noticed the only guys who ever seemed to get these girls were guys who responded to these girls with NO MOTION or MOTION AWAY.

One evening while watching this particular "Beautiful Tease" wreck her usual havoc upon all the men in the club, I just finally got it. I remember saying to myself, "You have to BE THERE and WITHDRAW. That's how you get that type of girl."

Now what I meant by that is that it was obvious to me that these women responded to MOTION AWAY. If you ignored them, they came and flirted with you. However, in a big club with hundreds of people, if you were truly going to apply MOTION AWAY how could I ever attract her? She would probably never see me, and if I walked away every time she approached me, how would I ever get her in bed?

That is when I realized that I had to BE THERE continually in close proximity to her, in order to communicate to her, and have a sexual relationship with her, but at the same time I had to WITHDRAW from her and make a MOTION AWAY from her continually to attract her and get her to want to be with me.

Within five minutes from having that realization, I came up with a motion pattern as a theory of how to deal with these girls, and within a few more hours, I had tested it out and concluded that it worked. (I got laid that night by the very girl I was watching.)

You see most guys would BE THERE all over the girl REACHING at her until she ran away. Then of course they would eventually get pissed off and WITHDRAW from the girl and want nothing to do with her, which would attract her and the whole cycle would start all over again because when she reached and flirted the pissed off guys would soften and think everything was OK and start reaching again.

I decided to be different from all these guys who REACHED then WITHDREW repeatedly in reaction to her flirtations. I came up with the decision and strategy to both REACH and WITHDRAW simultaneously.

My first REACH was to approach her indirectly (the indirectness puts withdraw into the reach). I did not directly walk up to her and start talking to her (that would have been pure reach) I walked up along side of her – shoulder to shoulder or a few feet apart and stood next to her within talking distance.

I then concentrated on WITHDRAW or motion away to pull her reach out of her. WITHDRAW was accomplished by 1) ignoring her and not hitting on her and 2) making comments out loud as if to myself about other hot women who walked by.

Ignoring her was not a strong enough withdraw to get her attention, but making comments about how hot other women were (and not noticing her) was not something this type of woman could bear. Invariably they would REACH and start a conversation with me about how guys always did the same thing to them.

Now if you go back and read my example in section 2 (c) again you will notice how I am using multiple channels here. I reach by being there PHYSICALLY. I withdraw by VERBALLY not communicating directly to her and paying attention to other women. I then REACH by engaging in a VERBAL conversation with her, but I simultaneously withdraw by VERBALLY communicating that I had no sexual interest in her (she was not my type) very politely but quickly.

Now I reinforced my verbal withdraw with other channels, I acted quite astonished with little facial expressions and all indicating disbelief when she told me how hot she was. MENTALLY I would even put forth a WITHDRAW by describing what my type was – and I would always describe it to be the opposite of whatever she was – if she was blonde, I liked brunettes. If she was flat-chested, I liked well-endowed women. If she was well endowed, I liked flat-chested women.

Now EMOTIONALLY however, I would always put forth a REACH or MOTION TOWARD by the end of our conversation. The EMOTIONAL REACH was always my closer.

The conversation was always about how hot she was and how odd it was that I was not attracted to her. About ten or fifteen minutes into the conversation, after she had told me for the third or fourth time how hot ALL guys considered her, I would say something like: “Are you sure guys like you for your looks. Don’t you think it might be that they just like you for your personality because I like your personality? You are really interesting. Maybe some of these guys you are meeting are just saying you are hot to make you feel good, but they really just like you for your personality."

Now that was the closer. That cinched the seduction. These girls had never had a guy say to them that he liked her for her personality. (Rightfully so, I guess, because most of these girls were out-and-out bitches.) This made me UNIQUE. A guy who liked them for their personality (REACH) but didn't want to have sex with them (WITHDRAW)

After this, the girl was mine. She was totally attracted to me and I had an excuse to BE THERE (I liked her personality) and this REACH didn't make her run away like it did with the other guys because I was not reaching sexually. Sexually I was still on a WITHDRAW which was totally attractive to her, and made her continually flirt with, and sexually REACH toward me.

All I had to do with these types of girls after this is continue to be there and let them make all the moves. They wanted to seduce me. All I had to do was let them. I had to keep up the WITHDRAW, by being slightly resistant (but willing for the sake of our friendship) never eager, never complimenting her physical or sexual aspects. I kept up my withdraw on all CHANNELS. Physically and verbally, I was slightly resistant, and never originated anything sexual. MENTALLY, I continue to communicate that they were not my type.

I REACHED emotionally, however, and by being there. I liked them as a friend. I liked their personality. That was communicated repeatedly. I was eager to see them and reached by simply BEING THERE.

I continued to do this before and even after we had sex. I could have kept these type of girls forever, as long as I didn't show them too much sexual reach. But in actuality this personality type quickly became boring to me.

So here is where we are. This is the core of my observational system. You have to OBSERVE motion in terms of REACH or MOTION TOWARD and WITHDRAW or MOTION AWAY and NO MOTION and PARALLEL MOTION upon occasion. And you have to observe it simultaneously across several communication channels – physical, verbal, emotional, mental, sexual, etc.

If you start making these observations you will begin to see what is going on in any situation and you will be able to extrapolate personality and situational types from this information and strategies to handle these personality and situational types will become apparent to you.

What is a situational type? Well a personality type might be a hot, friendly girl. But a situational type might be a hot, friendly girl who is on a date with another guy. These would require different strategies even though there is only one personality type you are dealing with here.

[The way you handle the above by the way is you approach the guy on a friendly guy vector (which is a way to be there on a WITHDRAW) but you say things to the guy which obviously the girl is going to hear that will attract her (REACH).]

When you are approaching a woman before you have developed a personality or situational strategy of your own, then you must pay close attention to MOTION across all the channels. Any information you can gather by observing her first is also helpful.

You must always make your adjustments to get MOTION or REACH toward you. Play around with the various patterns I have outlined above. Keep in mind that imitation is often effective (though imitation would not work with the "beautiful tease" in example 2 above). Adjust, adjust, and adjust until you get reach towards you. Then most importantly HOLD the REACH TOWARD you by continuing to do what you have done to create the reach on your end.

ONCE you get the reach, don't assume all is well, the girl likes you now and slip back into your old habits. YOU are CREATING the REACH, the ATTRACTION at all times – don't ever believe differently. If you stop creating it, it will disappear and you will lose the girl

Now naturally as her reach increases, the form of your reach will change too, but the basic pattern you work out will still be there. For example, the "beautiful teases" in EXAMPLE 2, some of them became my girlfriends for a while. Now I can't continue to say, "I am totally unattracted to you" after I start having sex with her. It is not logical and would be rude.

But what I absolutely don't ever do is say the truth – "You are sooooo hot. You are like the hottest girl I've ever seen and I just can't wait to jump you every night." Even though I am a big advocate of the truth, the "truth" is that would not work. I would have lost the girl very quickly if I ever did that.

So what I do is keep her being the aggressor. I can say things like, "I think I am becoming more attracted to you." "You know, I can see how some guys might think you are really hot."

And when she asks me about the sex, I don't say it was great. I say "it was okay, I just really enjoy being close and intimate with you. It gives me a special feeling inside."

No matter how the relationship evolves, with this personality type I will always have to use the combination of BE THERE and WITHDRAW. If I ever slip up and go into the total reach that I may feel, I will lose her fast. (Of course, this is not recognizing the fact that a few people can change and grow and change personality type. But as long as they remain the same personality type – which most people do - I will have to use the same basic strategy to create a successful relationship with them.)

Now as you begin to apply this personality technique, you won't always see the patterns in the very beginning. But you will make progress. You will start getting phone numbers. Girls will start calling you back. They'll want to kiss you after the first date rather than say, "I think we can be good friends."

It may take quite a bit of work to evolve the personality or situational strategy, but after you get a personality or situational strategy down it will usually work 80-90% of the time without fail. Moreover, the beauty is it is yours. It is your own personal strategy that works for you. Better yet, you are not limited to one strategy or one situation, but can start going after any personality type and situational type you so desire.

By simply observing motion you will eventually have the ability to go after and secure any type of girl you want and to obtain the type of relationship that you really want to create. You may get very skilled at seducing and getting a certain personality type as I did with the "beautiful teases" only to discover it is not the type for you.

That is okay, pick out another situation, another type, and learn how to create attraction with them. Keep doing this until you find the right type and the right girl for you.

Gradients

Now the final thing you need to observe may be the hardest, because it is not necessarily tangible. In fact most of the time it is intangible.

It is another one of those areas that women are more perceptive than men in. The area has to do with gradients.

Now I am going to go over gradients in greater detail in Chapter 9 (b) when I am talking about relationships more. However, it deserves a little bit of discussion at this time, as it will crop up from time to time in our dating technology.

Now what do I mean by "Gradient"?

Webster says a gradient is

"The rate of regular or graded ascent or descent"

Well perhaps Webster is falling a little short of a workable definition for our purposes.

For our purposes, let's just look at a "gradient" as a step on a ladder. Functionally a gradient allows us to safely go up the ladder or down the ladder one step at a time.

Now you have all been on a ladder and you know that ladders are quite workable and safe as long as you take it one step at a time. If you tried jumping up onto the fifth step of a ladder, you might have some problems getting there, and if you tried climbing or descending five steps at a time, well, you might just get hurt.

Now occasionally you could start on the second or third step of a ladder without any problem, and other times if you had some other means of ascending or descending (like your buddy lifts you up with a fork lift) you could get on or off a ladder at a higher step without any problem.

Get the picture? A gradient allows us to safely ascend or descend from one place to another.

Now when we are talking about developing or repairing or creating a relationship “gradients" are the steps that allow us to safely ascend to a higher level of relationship or safely descend (yes, there are times you have to do this too) to a lower level of relationship despite any opposition to our plan.

Gradients come into play immediately from the first time you meet a woman. Walking up to a woman you don’t know and saying “You are the most beautiful woman I have ever seen. Marry me.” Will usually be too high a gradient. Whereas “Hi” might work just fine.

Now the first thing you have to learn about gradients with respect to dating and relationships is how to see them. Gradients in dating and relationships are usually "mental" steps and as such are not as obvious as are the steps of a physical ladder.

This may be hardest thing about using gradients for guys to learn. Learning how to see them. Most people just don't observe much. They are too use to being told by others what is right and wrong, good and bad, and simply what is and isn't.

If you want to be successful at dating and relationships, YOU have to start observing gradients in respect to MOTION TOWARD and MOTION AWAY. Often you can turn a motion around by simply lowering the gradient. In my EXAMPLE 1 in Chapter 4(b) (iii), when I turn away from her and talk to her without facing her, I am LOWERING the gradient of my approach. (Indirect approach being a lower gradient of approach than direct approach.)

Also in EXAMPLE 2 with the “Beautiful Tease”, I close the deal by flirting with her on a LOWER GRADIENT. In fact in this case, I never move up to the gradient of telling her what a beautiful woman she is, because that is TOO HIGH a GRADIENT – even after we have had sex.

On the Sexual Scale that I outline in Chapter 4(b) (ii), each step is a gradient with “negative sex talk” being the lowest gradient I have observed for showing sexual interest.

This sexual scale was not something I was told. It was something I observed from mainly dealing with the “Gradient Girls” because with them, I had to step through every step on the scale and that is the order in which it went.

Most guys and people know what gradients are. We all know that intercourse is a higher sexual gradient than kissing. We all know that asking a girl out on a formal date is a higher gradient than asking her if she wants to hang out with you and your friends or get a cup of coffee.

The problem is NOT seeing a lower gradient when we need one. So when you walk up to a girl on a very low (you think) gradient and say “Hi.” And you scare the living daylights out of her. What do you do? What could be possibly lower than that?

Again, look at your channels of communication. When you said “hi”, did you walk up and face her directly? Were you smiling and obviously impressed by her looks? Lowering the gradient might not be verbal. You might say the same words “hi,” but while looking away from her with no expression on your face. She might then respond favorably.

Or perhaps lowering the gradient require that you change the verbal too. It might take an indirect verbal approach like the one I did with the “Beautiful Teases” in EXAMPLE 2. I didn’t say “hi” to her. I stood next to her and let her hear me talk to myself about other girls.

Get the idea?

When a person makes a motion away, the clever thing to do is find a lower gradient to come back on. Look at ALL the communication channels you are using and lower some or all of them to achieve the effect.

I'll talk more extensively about this in Chapter 9 (b), But for the time being know that it is one of the things that you must OBSERVE.

5) OBJECTIVES

Get Experience – Multiple or "Serial" Dating

When I wrote the eReport "How I Got 700 Dates in One Year," it caused a little controversy--usually amongst women.

Many women think that multiple or serial dating is a no-no, something that only dysfunctional people do. Well I got news for you. Everything is situational. Anyone that has followed my writings would know that that is my theme.

I would be the first one to agree that a person who "multiple" or "serial" dates with no intention of ever doing anything else would have at least some major "relating" issues.

But, serial dating applied in the right context is not only "not" dysfunctional, but it is quite the opposite. Serial dating done to get a better understanding of the opposite sex, so you can figure out who you like, and what you like, and what kinds of people like you, is about the most mentally healthy thing you can do.

What do you think most parents tell their teenage sons and daughters?

They tell them: "Don't get serious with one person; you need to date and meet a lot of girls/guys."

Now believe it or not, this teenage advice can also be very good advice for adults.

First of all, most adults never followed their parents' advice and dated lots of people. Most people seem to have a pattern of hooking up with the first "acceptable" person who shows them some real interest.

Unfortunately, there is a big difference between "acceptable" and "ideal" and also unfortunately most people usually continue this pattern of hooking up with the first "acceptable" person who comes along well into adulthood.

We call this "compromising" or "settling" and ultimately it leads to unhappiness in relationships, and a failure to understand the opposite sex.

You see there are many different types of people in the world and, believe-it-or-not, there is someone for everyone. But the problem is you may have to meet a hell of a lot of people to find that one someone.

Another problem is that many people are so confused about life and relationships and people, they don't really have any idea of what kind of personality is a good match for him/her. They base their ideals off the Hollywood imagery of what they think they want.

The cure is simple. When you date and meet lots of people, sooner or later you figure it out for yourself. It's a natural process. You get comfortable with people; you realize that everyone is different, and that different types of people like different types of people. Eventually you figure out what kind of person you are and what kind of people you get along with best.

Mom and Dad's teenage words of wisdom are good for everyone.

Now, I wouldn't advise anyone to go out of 700 dates in a year for the hell of it, not even 100 dates. However, if you want to understand the opposite sex and get a perspective on things, or if you just want to meet that person you've always been looking for, and then stop and settle down, "multiple" or "serial" dating might just be for you.

Sane Dating Principles Build Sane Relationships

I'm often asked if successful dating principles have anything to do with successful relationship principles.

My answer is always yes, definitely.

Dating activity is not a separate beast. Rather, exercising successful dating practices is a way to learn about and better understand women so that you can establish a good healthy relationship.

Dating is basically a time (or at least should be a time) when a person meets lots of people and formulates opinions and ideas about what kind of partner one gets along with best, is most productive with, and enhances or completes one's own abilities.

In order to do this, usually you have to meet a variety of people and see how it goes. Dating people doesn't necessarily mean you have to have sex with them, it just means you are going out with them, spending time with them, hanging out with them and getting to know them.

The most important dating principle of all is to meet and date lots of people. You know, it is what your mom and dad told you. Don't get serious with one person yet. Meet, lots of people.

Meet lots of people and talk about relationships and dating with the people that you meet. Get other people's perspective on "dating", “chemistry”, “relationships”, and any other thing you can. Particular attention should go to clearing up any confusions or worries you may have on any dating subject.

For example, I use to be very intimidated when a woman told me there was no "chemistry."

In my mind that meant I was "ugly" to her. I am a guy and because guys mainly think of chemistry in terms of physical attraction, I always thought that was what women were talking about when they used that term.

When I got divorced for the second time and realized I really didn't know everything I needed to know about relationships and women, I decided I needed to just meet a lot of women. I used online dating services and personal ads and being the "advertising guy that I am" I quickly developed a flow that accumulated about 50 phone numbers a week. I called about half of these people and ended up setting up and going on two dates a day for about a year.

Now when I started my adventure I had no idea I would be doing this for a year, but truth be told, I didn't meet anyone that I really liked, so I just kept at it until I did.

Lucky me.

Meeting a lot of people brings about a natural process of learning. And finally, when you meet someone you really like, you don't feel like dating anyone else, you just sort of stop pursuing "dating."

So, a year or so later, I had been on over 700 dates when I finally did meet someone and I settled down into what turned out to be a 7 year relationship.

During that year of intense dating, however, I learned more about women and understanding of women than I had ever learned previously in my whole life. Sure, I knew how to pick up a woman and get sex, but that doesn't really take a lot of understanding. I was looking for a more meaningful understanding of women. You know, what it takes to get married and live with someone day to day, happily, the rest of my life.

In fact, I abstained from sex that whole year. I didn't meet anyone I liked well enough to start a sexual relationship and I was already old enough to know that sex is a trap! When you start having sex with someone and they are the wrong person it is very easy to get trapped into that kind of a relationship, especially if it is almost a good relationship, then you'll work at it for a very long time as long as the sex is good.

It was from dating and just talking to 700 women, however, that I began to develop a real good perspective on what this whole relationship game was about.

Before going out on these 700 dates, I was intimidated by good looking women, afterwards I wasn't.

Before going out on these 700 dates, I always had sexual thoughts around any woman - good looking or not - afterwards I could look at a woman I wasn't interested in non-sexually - just as a friend. (Something women can do with men quite easily, by the way, but most men cannot reciprocate).

After going out on 700 dates I realized that there were a lot of women that I wasn't attracted to and had no desire to have sex with, that I still really liked as a person. Conversely, I learned that there were a lot of beautiful women who were pretty much "ugly" inside. And no matter how beautiful they are on the outside, I would never want to have sex with them.

So I came out of my year of 700 dates with the ability to be friends with a woman whose personality I liked without thinking or acting sexual around her. And with the ability to say "no" to a beautiful woman with a rotten or even mediocre personality.

Before this year of 700 dates, I was totally intimidated and invalidated as a being by a woman saying we didn't have "chemistry." (In the beginning I though chemistry was the same for women as it was for most men - physical attraction-- but it wasn't. Woman after woman told me stories of men that they had no or little physical attraction to, developing "chemistry" by what they said and did on that first or second date.)

At the end of my 700 dates, I understood the word "chemistry" from a female's perspective and started using it as a polite way of telling someone I wasn't interested in them.

Before my 700 dates I would automatically turn down a "hot" woman who applied for a nanny job. (I had the kids.) I didn't want the temptation and confusion of mixing interests between personal and business. At the end of my 700 dates, I was able to hire the "hottest" nanny you ever saw because she was simply the best woman for the job. I was no longer confused. I still didn't want to mix business and personal but was quite easily able to turn her down when she repeatedly offered herself to me late at night.

You see, before these 700 dates, even though I had the ability to go out to a club and get laid every night of the week, even though I had been married twice and in several long term relationships, even though I was the father of 2 children, I was -like most men- bewildered and confused and totally lacking confidence when it came to relating to and understanding a woman. Simply put they were foreign creatures - probably from Venus as the book says.

After my 700 dates, I was no longer confused. I realized that women were different than men in some ways, but in the most important way they were just like men.

And what way was that? - Personality.

Women just like men have varied and different personalities. They have rotten, mediocre, and great personalities just like men. And their personality types combine with their physical type to create ugly women with great personalities, ugly women with rotten personalities, ugly women with mediocre personalities, mediocre looking women with great personalities, mediocre looking women with mediocre personalities, etc. all the way up to probably every man's ideal of a great looking women with a great personality.

Now there is some kind of "normal curve" on this whole thing and the majority of women fall into the "mediocre looking women with a mediocre personality" range and the "hot looking woman with the great personality" is probably like the IQ 180 type - Rare!

The point is, however, that there is more variation between personality types than there is between sexes. Now I have talked about this earlier and I hope you get this because this is huge and most men don't get it.

The variations and differences between men and women are not as big a factor in the confusion regarding relationships, as are the variations and differences in personalities within both sexes.

So, guys, it is not that "All women are evil, cruel, and vicious." Some are and some aren't. It's just that you've been meeting the wrong ones.

So back to the point.

By meeting and dating lots of women you increase your chances of meeting someone on that normal curve who is in the same place as you. And when you do, the differences between men and women are small. It is when you meet a woman who is somewhere else on that "normal curve" of personality types, that it all becomes confusing. And the math of it all is that MOST women you meet are somewhere else on that curve.

What is the solution? The solution is to meet lots of women and find one that is on that same personality spot on the normal curve that you are.

Meeting and dating a lot of people is the most basic principle because it leads to self evident truth. If you just meet a lot of people (The exact number may be different for each person. For me it was 700. For someone else it may be 50. For yet another it may be 2000.) There comes a point where you naturally learn something about women and people and yourself. The natural learning you get for yourself is senior to and much better than anything I or anyone else can tell you vicariously. It also is directly applicable to you and your situation.

Other dating principles that came out of that "700 dates" experience are the following.

1) Remember that there are different personalities you will be dating and that different personalities require different interaction. Don't ever be stuck with just "one way" of interacting with women. Try different things and see what works. Always look at what you do to cause a person to move closer or what you do to cause them to move further away. Sometimes the same action on your part has almost opposite reactions on different personality types. If you observe this, you will know when to do what.

2) Use the dating experience to develop a concept of your "ideal woman." When I noticed a quality - either physical or mental or emotional - that I really liked about a woman I would write it down. I would also write down qualities that I didn't like - qualities that irritated me and that I was uncomfortable with.

From these lists of qualities I liked and didn't like, I eventually developed and "ideal" for the woman I would like to marry. I now know the exact qualities I would want her to have and not have - no confusion. This is what the dating experience is for. Getting to know people and yourself. Use it!

3) "Don't compromise your integrity" is another major dating principle. Men and women continually compromise their integrity when they are in a scarcity condition. A guy doesn't meet women. Then he meets one woman who lives down the hall from him. They start hanging out and they have sex. Then she turns into a bitch and he can hardly stand her but he likes the sex, so he puts up with it although it irritates him. Occasionally or frequently, they get in fights over things because of personality clashes.

When you are meeting lots of people it is a lot easier not to sacrifice your integrity. If someone starts acting weird, you drop them knowing there is plenty more where that came from.

4) When you are dating and meeting lots of people it also helps if you are a non-jealous person. Actually, meeting a lot of people helps you develop into a "non-jealous" person. When you see how meeting lots of people increases your certainty on knowing what kind of person you want, you don't discourage others from doing the same.

I actually prefer meeting a girl who has met and gone out on a lot of dates. I want a girl who picks me out of 100 guys and says "you are the one I want." I much prefer that to some girl who has led a sheltered life and only has gone out with me. Even if I am perfect for her, she (due to lack of experience) may not know that. Someday she may break up with me just to find out what it is like to be with another man.

When someone has checked out a lot of people, has her choice of dozens of men, and chooses me, I don't have that problem.

Don't be jealous. Encourage others you are dating to go out with other people. If it is right, it will happen despite anything.

I have never asked a girl to be exclusive with me. What happens is when you really meet someone you like, you just don't want to see other people any more. Without even asking, you both start just seeing each other exclusively.

One day you turn to her and you say. "I'm not seeing anyone else anymore. Are you?" and she says "No?" That is the way it happens naturally and the way it should be. You Shouldn't have to ask a person to be exclusive. If it is right, it just happens.

5) It is also important while dating that you don't get needy. There is a principle here that is totally true. If after meeting some people, you kind of get along and start hanging out together, remember, while dating, you shouldn't go out with a person more than once or twice a week if you want to maintain a "dating" relationship.

If you start going over to the girl's house every night or 3 or 4 times a week, or even start calling a girl every night and talking on the phone, you are acting like a boyfriend and she will start treating you like one. You will be out of the dating stage and into the boyfriend/girlfriend stage whether you like it or not. Whether you intend to do so or not.

So don't be needy. If you are lonely, go out with another girl. I can't tell you how many times this saved me from "false love." False love is when you meet someone and you emotionally feel like you are in love and they are just perfect (even though you really don't know them yet.) Usually what is going on is that you are just emotionally needy and they have some quality on the surface that you really like.

These are the kinds of relationships that trap you. Because they seem like heaven at first but eventually turn into hell. The problem is you didn't really get to know the person. You were just emotionally needy. And they were on their "good' or social behavior while they were trying to "get you." After they feel they have you, they then feel safe enough to be themselves and they turn into a demon of some sort. I am sure you have been through one of these. Most of us have.

Whenever I feel "I am in Love." I make a point to meet and go out with others. If my love is real, it will still be there in 3 weeks or 3 months. If it is not and only "false love" seeing others keeps my perspective on things and I begin to notice little things about her that aren't so great (compared to others) and the false love disappears and I let go a "sigh" of relief, knowing I dodged yet another bullet.

6) Another major principle when dating with the purpose of finding the right girl and developing a long-term relationship is not to get involved in sex too quickly. Find out how and what a girl feels about sex before you do the deed. Have fun making out and petting but just don't go all the way.

Having sex is used by a lot of personality types (both men and women) as a trap. If you have sex with them, then you are their boyfriend/girlfriend. So be careful - not needy. I tend to always have a sexual partner (this is a sex-only type relationship where you both just have fun and aren't looking to take it any further) when I am dating and looking for a serious relationship and meeting lots of people. This allows me to meet people without being needy and keeps me out of the trap if there is one.

These are basic "dating" principles that will allow you to meet lots of people, help you define what it is you like, dislike and are looking for in a woman, keep your integrity to yourself in tack, and eventually help you find that special person you are looking for.

Use them wisely!

Now in the next section, I will explain how these same principles can be applied to an existing relationship for betterment. (No, I am not going to have you go out and meet 700 women while you are married. But I will show you how the principle behind meeting 700 people can be applied to one person to better the relationship!)

Sane Dating Principles Can Be Applied to Existing Relationships

In the last section, we went over successful dating principles and I told you I would tell you how to apply these successful "dating principles" to relationships.

1) So let us take the most important principle of dating - meeting lots of people.

What does this possibly have to do with relationships? Obviously, you are not going to go out and meet women on "dates." So how is this applied?

Let's look at the purpose of meeting lots of people while dating.

The purpose of meeting and dating many people is to learn about the other sex, and yourself with respect to what you like and do not like in partners.

You do that through communication and observation.

By communication, you can, for example:

1) Tell people what you think and get their responses, reactions.
2) Tell people what you like and get their responses, reactions.
3) Tell people the kind of relationship you are looking for and get their reactions.
4) Find out what other people think on a certain topic.
5) Find out what women like in men.
6) Find out what women expect from men.
7) Find out what sort of agreement a woman is looking for.
8) Find out what sort of relationship a woman is looking for.
9) Find out if you have things in common.
9) Find out what is on their mind. What sort of things do they bring up and talk about with you.

By observation, you can determine:

1) A persons emotions - where are they at most of the time? Are they angry, sad, happy?
2) A persons production level - do they get a lot done or are they lazy?
3) Their habits, routines - are they a slob? Neat freak? etc.
4) Do they keep their agreements with people?
5) Are they moving closer toward you or moving away from you mentally, emotionally, physically, and/or sexually?
6) Are they an affectionate or cold person?

These lists of communications and observations can go on and on, but above are some examples of things you might want to communicate about and observe when you first meet and start dating a person.

The point is when dating and meeting people we are not doing that just for the heck of it. (At least you shouldn't be.) You are doing it to learn about people. To qualify prospects and to find someone who is compatible with you.

After you have talked to and observed enough people, you naturally start seeing how things work - what you like and don't like, what women, in general are looking for, etc.

Without this experience, most people (not all) are usually confused about the opposite sex, yet needy, and make judgment mistakes simply because they don't have a lot of choices.

Their need to have a sexual relationship overrides their need for understanding. So they often compromise their integrity and get involved in something they deep down know they shouldn't (with the hope or prayer that they can change the situation or person eventually.)

Often these people end up learning the hard way after years and years of bad experiences in a bad relationship.

So in a relationship you still have the same purposes as dating, but with a few substitutions. Instead of learning about how women work, and what you like and dislike about women, and what women like and dislike about men in general; you want to learn how a particular woman works, and what you like and dislike about her and what she likes and dislikes about you in particular.

What makes her move closer to you –emotionally, mentally, physically, sexually? What makes her move away from you?

So when you are in a relationship you are going to go out on not "700 Dates" with 700 different women (a joking reference to my dating eBook- "How I Got 700 Dates In One Year"). You will go out on 7000 or even 30,000 or more dates with the same woman. But the purpose on each one of those dates is the same as when you were meeting and dating many different women. The purpose is to get to learn about her and get to know her better each time you spend time with her. This should NEVER end.

Communication and observation. Every time you spend time with your girlfriend or your wife, you have to treat it a little bit like it was a first date. Ask her questions, observe her reactions. Find new territory that you've never discussed before. Ask those questions that you are a little afraid to ask. Don't take her for granted. People are infinitely complex and ever changing.

By doing this continually, you will be able to learn about and understand and know your partner better and better continually. You will then be able to use "gradients" to improve and create the relationship as I discuss in Chapter 9 (b).

So when dating you are learning about women and yourself in order to qualify and select the right woman for you. In a relationship, you are learning about a particular woman to be able to create the relationship in the direction you would like it to go.
The more you learn the easier it gets.

Occasionally, however, you might learn that you are in a relationship with the wrong woman for you. If that is the case, it is usually best to end it and start over again. It is usually not a good idea to compromise your integrity for anyone. Children need good role models. And children are definitely not happy being brought up in a household without love, or worse yet, one with arguing and bickering all the time.

2) Now how do we use the second dating principle "Use the dating experience to develop a concept of your ideal woman." in a relationship?

Well you are pretty much going to do the same thing. Write down the qualities that you really like in your partner and write down the qualities that you don't like. In a relationship, you have to continually confront both the positive and the negative.

Reinforce the positive qualities - If you like it when your wife wears make-up and does her hair. Make a big deal about it every time she does it. Tell her how beautiful she looks. If she gets positive reinforcement, I guarantee you she will do it more often. Don't ever take a woman (or anyone) for granted. If you take things for granted, they will soon disappear

Whatever you have on your like list - reinforce it, compliment it, acknowledge it continually and it will remain and get even better.

Now the things you don't like, use "gradients" to change. (See: Chapter 9(b)).

Also, be willing to trade. If she eats popcorn in bed and it irritates the hell out of you, well, be willing to give up reading that magazine on the toilet that irritates the hell out of her.

When dating we used this principle to develop an "ideal" of the kind of woman we would want to have a relationship with. When in a relationship we use this principle to create that ideal with the woman we are with.

3) Don't compromise your integrity is another major dating principle that applies to relationships as well. Sometimes we have to tell our little "white lies" to not hurt another's feelings, but when the choice comes down to "compromising your integrity" or "hurting another's feelings" it is usually better NOT to compromise your integrity.

If not compromising your integrity leads to a breakup, then it wasn't the right relationship for you. Be honest and open in your communications with your partner, don't be afraid to tell them how you really feel about things. In the end if you stick with your integrity, it will all work out for the best for everyone.

Always keep your word. That is a part of integrity. A man or woman really doesn't have more much than their word that people can count on. If your word is worthless, than so are you.

4) When you are dating and meeting lots of people it also helps if you are a non-jealous person. That still applies if you are in a healthy relationship. It is actually good for men and women to have friends of the opposite sex; as long as they are monogamous people and have worked through all their tendencies to not be monogamous, it can actually help a healthy relationship to have opposite-sex friends.

If you have the right girl or guy and you hang for a little while with someone who is not right, all it does is make you appreciate your partner even more and NOT take them for granted.

This issue totally depends on you having worked through jealousy issues in the dating stage. If you haven't, you may not be able to do it in a relationship. And certainly, if you realistically can't trust your spouse (because of past transgressions, etc.) than jealousy and opposite-sex friends may not be something you can easily resolve. And it may not even be a good idea to try.

5) Even in relationships, it is also important, as in dating, that you don't get needy - but in a different way. Obviously, you are going to see the person more than once or twice a week. But make sure you have your own life. Don't depend on your partner for your own existence.

Be able to do things apart and separate from each other. Be able to be in the same room without needing to talk or interact. Be able to do your own thing while together. Men should never force their sexual needs on a woman - that will make sex quite an unenjoyable experience for both of you very quickly.

Women are actually much more sexual creatures than men, but what turns them on and gets them n the mood isn't the same as for men. Men are also in the mood much more quickly.

If men don't understand the differences between men and women sexually, both partners (including younger women who often feel they don't like sex that much simply because they have not had a good male sex partner that knew how to prepare them for sex, or give them an orgasm) may get the impression that the female is not into sex. (See Chapter 12 (b) "How To Get Your Wife or Girlfriend To Want More Sex.")

6) And the last dating principle - don't get involved in sex too soon- can be also utilized as a relationship principle with a slight modification. Don't get involved in "intercourse" too quickly - and that can be applied every time you have sex.

Women need foreplay. Give it to them. You'll be a better lover and you will also enjoy sex more if you get into foreplay. There is a lot more to sex than an orgasm. If you are a guy and you haven't figured that one out yet, there is a lot more information about this on our website, www.DatingToRelating.com. Use it.

Prospecting and Qualifying - Is She the Girl You Are Looking For?

Prospecting and Qualifying are two basic sales or pre-sales technology terms.

Nevertheless, prospecting and qualifying have a continuing role in dating and in established relationships.

Most guys don't apply prospecting and qualifying to dating because they don't know enough women. Well, that is what prospecting is about. Developing potential leads of women who could possibly be a relationship for you.

I have even seen guys who can meet all kinds of women fail miserably at prospecting. They are not shy. They talk to women left and right, but they fail miserably at prospecting and qualifying because they have no idea what a prospect is.

Let's define some of these "sales" terms so we can use them in our dating and relating analogy.

A "lead" in sales is usually someone who you can communicate to (by mail, phone, in person) to see if they are actually a "prospect" - a prospect being someone who has certain identifiable features that makes it more likely than the usual lead that they would be interested in what you have to offer; and a "hot prospect" is ready, willing and able to act upon what you have to offer now.

So if you are selling solar roofing panels, a list of people who own their own homes (as opposed to a list of renters) might be leads that you mail to. A hot prospect might be someone who has high-energy bills, is looking to save money and lower monthly outgo, has equity in their home to finance the purchase without a penny out of their pocket, someone who is environmentally conscious and is ready to do this now.

Salesmen are trained to approach a lead and establish very quickly by a series of questions (qualifying) if a person is actually a prospect or not. You maximize your Return on invested time (as a salesmen) by spending only a couple of minute on a person who is not a qualified prospect thereby saving your time consuming pitch and energy for the few people who are prospects. On the average a good salesman might only spend 2 minutes with a non-qualified lead, and 20 to 60 minutes with a qualified prospect.

Another basic principle of sales is that sales is a numbers game. The more leads you talk to, the more prospects you get. The more prospects you get, the more sales you close.

Now all of the above applies directly to dating and relating.

I have talked about meeting many women in previous Chapters so I will not go into that topic much here. However, just make a note, to get the most out of prospecting when meeting women; you need to meet lots of women.

But there is plenty you can do to mess up after that.

Now most guys naturally do what they think is prospecting -- Is she single? Is she cute?

Most of us guys know to find out the answers to those questions before we go on to wasting our time and energy. That is really not prospecting. It is just sorting out the leads (someone you should to talk to) from those you should not bother to talk to.

And by the way, I would add to the basic "Is she a lead list" Is she moving toward you, or away from you? Because if she is not interested in you and moving away from you, you are wasting your time (unless you know the art of seduction - which is another lesson to be found in a later Chapter 10.)

Now once you do your basic sort and decide which girls you should talk to, this is where prospecting really begins.

How does she feel about relationships? What is she looking for? What kind of relationship is she looking for? What kind of guy is she looking for? What does she expect from a guy in a relationship.

Is she affectionate? Does she like to cuddle at night? Does she like sex? How often? Does she want children? How many?

Is she smart? How smart? Is she educated? How educated? What kind of career does she want? How important is it to her? What is more important to her family or career? What is more important to her? Her husband or her friends? Her children or her husband? Her mother or her husband?

What is her family like? How does she handle her family? Is she still a little girl afraid to stand up to mom, dad, aunt and uncle? Or has she grown up and able to command respect from her elders?

What is her personality like. Is she warm or cold? Is she happy most of the time or sad? Is she stable or up and down? Is she augmentative, or does she like to resolve problems? Is she basically crazy or basically sane?

Is she a neat freak or a slob? Is she mellow or uptight? Is she easy going or a hard-ass?

There are hundreds of more questions. The list just goes on and on.

However, in order to figure out if someone is a good prospect for you, you have to ask questions, and like the salesman, you have a choice. You can qualify someone in two minute (or two dates, or two months in our case) or waste a lot of time on them by going into your sales pitch, just to find out in the end they weren't a prospect after all. (In our case that might be 2 or 3 years of relating to find out what you could have found out in two months of intense qualifying and prospecting "communicative dating" in the beginning.)

Not only do you qualify when you first meet a woman, as you move along in relationships you have to continually qualify women especially as you move from level to level of relationship.

The girl who is a hot lover, may make a lousy girlfriend. The girl who was an excellent see-you-three-times-a-week girlfriend may make a terrible "roommate' when you finally chose to live together. The girl who was a good "roommate" or living together partner, may make a crummy wife and mother.

Every type of relationship has its own set of unique qualifying questions and answers. Every guy has his own unique set of questions and answers for each type of relationship.

So you see, when you are eighteen "Is she cute?" and "Does she have a boyfriend?" may seem to be the only two questions you need answered. But unless you are extraordinarily lucky, it won't be enough. And it is NOT qualifying or defining a prospect. It is only defining a lead.

Now oddly enough, there is one physical attribute you can immediately notice about a person that can act as a qualifier. It correlates 80-90% with personality. And that of course is the “feet angles” I discussed previously in Chapter 3(c).

But let's move on.

You see in order to prospect, you actually have to know what a good prospect is in order to ask the right questions. A salesman learns the hard way that people without money, jobs, or good credit will listen to his sale pitch all day and he'll never make a sale. So he learns very quickly to qualify people for job, money, or good credit in those first two minutes. If they don't have any of the three, then he is gone (very politely and very quickly) if he is a good salesman.

This is where the experience factor comes in. By meeting lots of women (like the salesman who meets people over and over again every day) you learn quickly what you like and what you don't like. What makes a woman a good prospect or a bad one? What makes you a good prospect to a woman or a bad one?

Now when you first start compiling this list of likes and dislikes, it can be quite a challenge. I think my personal list got up to about 50 attributes at one time. But, fortunately, you start noticing similarities between attributes and that some attributes create others and it comes back down again to 4, 5, or 6 real basic things that you really need in a woman to have any kind of a decent chance at having a successful life long relationship with a woman.

And believe me, when you know this, you know yourself.

When you then qualify and find a woman who has all of these basic characteristics, you have a real prospect.

So now do you stop prospecting and qualifying?

No, never.

You must continue to ask those questions and qualify a woman as you are dating and relating to her. You must continue to define what she is looking for as well as what you are looking for the rest of your life. Things change and you must be willing to change with them or let go of them.

Even our salesman in the TV store understands this. If suddenly, one day, 90% of the people who walk into his store want big screen TVs, even if he's never carried them he adjusts and changes and starts carrying them. Why? Well because he wants to sell TVs and if that is what his customers want, he wants to give them what they are looking for.

Same for a man. When you meet women as you are dating and 90% of them say they want a "well dressed' gentleman as a boyfriend, well you'd have to be an idiot not to go buy some new clothes and reads some books to improve your manners. (But then again there is always "integrity' and if this is really not for you, then better to concentrate on the 10% of women who are not looking for that - but at least now you will know what to qualify your prospects for - someone who is NOT into "well dressed gentlemen.")

The point is, things change. So the qualifying questions and communication never ends. You do it the rest of your life, you make decisions to change and move forward or retreat, and end cycle based on those answers.

When the wife of thirty years suddenly says she is bored with everything you have been doing for the last 30 years, well, it just might be time to bring in the "big screen" TV, or you might find your wife shopping elsewhere.

Get it. Ask questions. Listen to the answers.

6) TURN MEETING AND DATING INTO RELATIONSHIPS

Creating "Future"

Future is an interesting but very overlooked dating and relating concept.

Future is the essence of a relationship. It is the "why" in "Why we have a relationship."

If we didn't care about future, our dating and love life would be different.

We would simply wake up in the morning, go about our life and randomly hook up with someone for some romantic pleasure, then go our merry ways respectively.

While there are a few people who do live their lives this way, most of us care about future. We want to hook up with someone romantically that we can also hook up with in the future repeatedly.

Most of us are concerned with future, and yes, it is the driving force behind the concept of a relationship, yet it is seldom talked about and there is little education on this topic with respect to dating and relationships.

So let's break the mold and start addressing it. Because understanding and creating "future" makes meeting women, picking up women, attracting women, and relating to women much less difficult.

All of these activities, start, survive, and end on the concept of future. But it is key to remember that it is not just future alone, it is "future" mixed with acceptable activity in the future. And all the other techniques I have talked to you about - such as gradients - need also be applied to future.

Even though you could walk up to a strange woman and say, "Do you want to go to my place in 10 minutes and have sex?" And even though that would be creating a future, it would not be (most often) creating acceptable activity in the future.

Seduction is the art of using "future" and gradients to create acceptable future activity leading to a goal. So asking a girl out to dinner, having great conversation, some hand holding at the movie, back to your place for a nightcap, some kissing...well this will lead to the same place but will work much more often and with more women than the other technique.

But the other techniques - do you want to go to my place and have sex - IS creating future and will actually work a small percentage of times (1 out of 100 -1000). And the guy who did that would be more successful than the guy who talks to women, creates no future, then just walks away.

So let's start with talking about how future can be applied to "meeting" women and even "picking up" women.

If you don't have "creating a future" as a target in mind when you begin this kind of activity in can be a mistake. You can randomly talk to a woman, establish no future, and then just walk away when the conversation is over. This would be a mistake and you would leave with some sort of odd feeling of “I wonder if I should have said…I wonder if I should have asked her…”

When you are trying to meet or "pick up' women, make your job easier. Have some attention on future and a goal to walk away with an agreement to contact each other again in the future for some reason.

The most obvious way to establish future is to ask a girl out on a date. But when it comes to strangers walking down the street, well it might work on "not-so-hot-chicks" but definitely does not work on "really hot chicks" as they get asked out about 15 times a day every day. They also get tired of guys just being interested in them for their body.

So with hot girls the goal is to establish future without seeming like you are only interested in their body. Best way to do this is to engage them in some sort of conversation, find an area of mutual interest, then find something they are really interested in that you know, and say you will email them or call them with some information on it.

Since you are not focusing on how "hot" and sexy they are, they will most always accept and/or return your call or email.

Probably the hardest task of all is to stop some hot chick walking the opposite way from you dead in her tracks, engage her in a conversation, and establish some future with her. To do it you have to do it gradiently - one step at a time. Like stop her and ask her for the time or directions, then notice something interesting about her. Like, "Where did you get that watch? My sister's been looking for one just like it. Do you mind if I write this down? Hey, you know another good place is..." or “Wow, that's a neat cell phone. Do you like it? Mine is a piece of junk...So is my service….What service do you have?” etc.

The point is always to end this gradient conversation with you having some information - name of a store, etc - that she would really be interested in that you cannot remember right now, but that you can get from your sister, or you have it written at home, etc...which gives you a good reason to call her in the future to give her the information.

Now of course she knows you are really calling because you are interested in her, but if you do it this way, she won't feel like a piece of meat, she'll think you have some class, and she'll answer the phone, or call you back when you leave a message.

Another way to apply "future" to "meeting" and "picking up" women, is to make it easier on yourself to begin with. As I said, the situation above is one of the hardest to tackle successfully. But the easiest thing to do is to try to meet or pick up women in situations with "future" built in.

For example, going to the mall, and checking out all the women who work there gives you a "future" advantage. They work there. They'll be there again tomorrow, next week, etc. So here you don't have to stop her dead in her tracks and have this insanely clever conversation.

When a girl works somewhere and you know how to see her again, a simple smile or flirt will do. You can have a conversation without pushing it all the way to asking for a phone number.

The fact that you can smile, or flirt, or have a simple conversation and come back multiple times without taking it all the way, means to a woman that you are checking her out, that you have standards, that her personality is just as important as her looks. You won't even make a move until you thoroughly check out her personality. Women like that. Makes you romantic, and mysterious. They'll start wondering - will he, or won't he?

Situations with built in future give you the advantage over the street and clubs and other random places where you may never see the person again.

You need to know how to handle both situations to be successful however. You never know when or where you might meet "Miss Right."

When you focus is on picking up women in a club or a bar for an immediate future like a one-night-stand, you need to plan intermediate future goals to achieve your purpose.

When you walk up to a girl in a club or bar you should have something like this in mind for the future: She will pair off with you exclusively, then want to go somewhere else with you, then want to make out with you, go home with you, etc.

So you simply have these points in mind and watch what is going on and know when to take it to the next level. So when she pairs off with you exclusively (the first good sign of interest), take it to the next level. Say let's go to the back room (where you can make out) it's more cozy. Or say let's go to the club down the street - better music. Or do you want to get something to eat? (Which can be a prelude to making out in the car.) Or saying let's go to my place for a night-cap….get the picture?

If you don't have these future activity points thought out and in mind before the approach you might blow what otherwise could be a very lovely evening.

Future continues to play a role in relationships as relationships develop. On a first date, I always look to see if a woman tries to establish future with me. If she does, then I know she likes me. I also try to establish a little bit of subtle future with her, or better yet try to get her to establish future with me as the date progresses.

Rather than asking a girl if you can go out again at the end of a date (and missing all the clues the whole time) it is better to get her signals and give your own throughout the date. And it is MUCH better to mix your future with a common interest, rather than having everything focus on just going out with her again. Everyone wants future, but no one wants future with some obsessive, clingy person.

So if the conversation, for example, gets around to a mutual interest, like say Bruce Willis movies, and there is a new Bruce Willis movie coming out next week, that is the time to say, "Hey, you want to catch the movie together? It would be fun seeing the movie with someone who likes him as much as I do."

The biggest thing about establishing future is doing it right. Guys know they have to establish future with a girl. But telling some stranger she is hot, and asking her out on a date doesn't work most of the time (it does work some of the time depending on the girl) and especially doesn't work with hot girls. Because it gives the girl the impression (rightfully so) that the guy is only interested in sex.

So when the purpose of establishing future is obviously sex - most girls don't like it. When the purpose of establishing future is to obviously check her out because you might like her if she has a nice personality and common interests - most girls love it. That's what girls do. That is what they understand. You'll score big if you do it this way.

So that is the theme in those first few dates leading up to getting intimate. Once you are intimate, the future factor changes. And the emphasis in the second stage of dating (post intimacy) is establishing just how much future and what quality future do you want to have with this person. - Daily future, twice a week future, once a week future, etc. Lovers' future, boyfriend/girlfriend future, no commitment future, marriage future.

The kind of future at this stage that no one usually wants is the clingy "I just want to be with you" future with no other interests or commonality defined.

Now if you want to have a good relationship it is important to be honest with yourself and your partner at this stage and really define for them the kind of future you really want, and get them to define for you the kinds of future they really want. If you fail to do that early on, you can fall into an undefined relationship that is too comfortable to leave, but not comfortable enough to marry.

Not where you want to be….where you want to be is to clearly define for your partner what kind of future you are looking to create and have them clearly define for you what kind of future they are looking to create. If your futures meet, you stand a better chance of making it in the future. If you are not creating the same future, then better to move on while you can, or redefine the relationship as lovers, or friends or some such relationship that has no romantic future that is just enjoying the present for however long it lasts.

Now when you finally take the plunge and you are boyfriend/girlfriend, living together, married, or even in a non-traditional relationship such as lovers or friends with privileges, etc., you must sill create future. Again the quality of the future create will shift.

Once you have committed to a relationship and the future is no longer mysterious and the conversation and create is no longer centered around "will we get married?" etc., you still can't take a person for granted. Just because they said they would be there forever and ever amen, doesn't mean they will -even though they meant it when they said it.

About the only mistake you can make, once committed, is to take someone for granted and to stop creating future with and for them. So all that stuff you did to create future with and for her to get her, is all the stuff you still must continue doing to keep her in the future.

If you keep that attitude, you will have a successful relationship.

Perhaps the topic of "future" activities together might change. Perhaps now it is talk about future children, future career, future houses, boats, and cars. Or future grandchildren, future retirement, future travel, etc. Still the little future things that got you started should not stop. So "hey - new Bruce Willis film out tomorrow" should still be there. (or if not Bruce, then your new mutual acting hero.)

The point is keep putting future there the rest of your life. No matter how many years you've been married or lovers or whatever. Keep putting it there. Don't take things for granted, don't get patterned in the past, don't get stale. Keep creating the future and putting it there with and for your partner.

Yes, you now know that this girl WILL have sex with you. But that doesn't mean you cut to the chase. Seduce her, treat her like you would treat a first, second or third date. Take her down a path of futures. A little hugging, a dinner, cuddle while you watch TV, a little kissing and then....The future will be more enjoyable for the both of you.

And just like the guy walking down the street, or shopping for "girls" in the mall, you'll stand a better chance of survival.

Finally, when you are continually creating future in a relationship, it gives you a source of feedback from your partner about their changes over time. When you put something out there for the future that she use to enjoy and she says no, that means she is changing or she wants something different. So you learn about your partner, and you change with her and create new things (or if she doesn't go in a direction you want to go then you talk about it and if it's the right thing you go your separate ways).

Just like you assess the girl on the first date to find out if she is the girl for you and how to create a relationship with her, You continually assess your girlfriend or wife of many years by continually putting future out there for her to react to - so you can find out if she is still the girl for you and to know how to create an even better relationship with her.

Meeting Women Walking Down the Street

I've been asked by quite a few guys to give specific strategies on how to pick up women in random situations like walking down the street, in grocery stores, in restaurants etc.

As I have said before meeting women that you can actually see has its advantages over internet and classified meetings. Thus, meeting women on the street - stores, malls, parks, concerts, events, the beach, grocery stores, Starbucks, etc. - allows you to see the real deal. You can see what they look like without being victim to the 10-year-old pictures that you find on the internet, and you can see what their personality is like without being disguised by internet dribble-drabble.

It is one of my favorite ways to meet women but it is something I have to do when I have a lot of time because pound for pound meeting women on the street successfully is much more time intensive than internet and classified advertising. (And by successfully, I don't mean just getting a phone number. Lots of guys can do that to no avail. I mean turning a meeting on the street into a girlfriend, a lover, a relationship!)

It can also be one of the hardest ways to successfully meet women, depending on the situation. Ninety-nine percent of the hot women that I have dated have told me they would never go out with a guy who approaches them on the street no matter how good looking and cool he was.

But if you seriously want to be a skilled craftsman at meeting women, meeting them on the street is something you definitely have to master. Once you master it "Where to meet women" becomes a rather mute point. As you will be able to meet women anytime, anywhere, any place.

However, there is a different approach you have to take with street-meetings when the goal is to establish a relationship. If you just want to flirt or get a phone number you can do things entirely different. You can out-and-out flirt or be cocky-and-funny, etc.

The first thing that matters is the QUALITY of the girl you are going after. HOT women get hit up upon all the time on the street. They are much less responsive to street techniques and as stated above most of them feel they would never have a serious relationship with a guy they met on the street.

The strategies I am going to give you below are designed for HOT women. Keep in mind that if you are interested in women not quite as hot, you can in general be more aggressive with flirting and flattery.

There are two basic strategies I have used when "street shopping" by myself.

1) The out-an-out-flirt technique. You approach a woman on a flirt and if she is unresponsive, you move on.
2) The gradient no-flirt technique.

There are also four basic situations I encounter when "Street Shopping."

1) Stopping a woman who is walking on the street, in a mall, store, etc.
2) Approaching a woman who is relatively stationery in a store, library, grocery store, etc.
3) Approaching a woman who works in a store, etc. and who will be there again.
4) Approaching a woman who is walking, while you are driving in a car.

Ok, so let's start with Situation 1 - Stopping a woman who is walking on the street, in a mall, etc.

Now, this is usually the hardest kind of pick-up of all. The woman is not in a situation that she is looking to meet anyone. She is walking and has other things on her mind. You only have a matter of seconds to pull it off. And she may be married or in a serious relationship and not interested

This is a situation in which I would never use out-and-out flirt techniques, unless the woman flirts with me first. Remember, hot women don't think much of men who flirt with them on the street. It is obvious to them that the only reason the guy is approaching them is because of their looks, because the guy obviously doesn't know anything else about them.

(Conversely, if a girl is not-so-hot she would be much more open to flirting leading to a serious relationship because she doesn't get guys hitting on her AT ALL for her looks.)

What I use in this situation is usually the gradient no-flirt technique. Usually I have to mentally prepare for this depending on where I am. I have a series of questions thought out ahead of time that I can ask a woman in a situation, that are situationally and socially acceptable.

So say I am in the mall, for example. I am walking down the aisle and I see a very hot woman approaching me. Now before hand I have thought out several strategies that I can approach her with, like:

1) Her clothes - My buddy had to go out of town on an emergency and asked me to pick up something for this new girl he is dating. She loves clothes. I notice that you a sharp dresser. I like your style. I have good taste, but I have no clue where to buy clothes like that. Where would you suggest I go shopping around here?

Now this will not be perceived as a flirt, but a cry for help, by the woman I approach. At the same time, I DO compliment her and make her feel good about her personality because I am basically saying I like her style and think she dresses well. Another factor that is good about this approach is it creates time - a conversation rather than a quick answer. It is a lot better than approaching a woman and saying, "Do you know where BEBE is?"

Now the above is the concept not the patter. I talk slow and deliberate with confidence and say it however it feels comfortable.

Also notice that I make it known I am shopping for my Buddy's girlfriend which gives her the impression that I may be single and also subtly lets her know that I am NOT a slime ball cheating on my own girlfriend. (If she eventually perceives I am flirting with her.)

2) Her smell - Again I am shopping for my buddy who is out of town on an emergency or for my Mom (easier to do this with perfume than clothes) and I notice she had a really nice smelling perfume on. What is it? Where can I get it? She obviously has good taste in perfumes. Are there any other perfumes she would recommend?

3) If all else fails and I can't think of anything. I will fall back on an old standby. I will ask if she knows what time it is. This is much harder because it is not a conversation. It is a question and answer. It only creates a few seconds of interaction. So the second part of this is to notice something about her in the three seconds that you have while she is giving you the time. Like "Wow" what a cool watch. Where did you get that?" Or "Wow, those are really neat shoes." Or "What cool earrings?"

Now the point of all these strategies is to get into communication with the woman on a non-flirting vector. She sees me as a guy just looking for some help. This is VERY important because now the HOT woman WILL consider me a prospect for a relationship even though she met me on the street, because I am NOT some random guy just hitting up on her for her looks.

The point of creating a conversation is twofold. It creates TIME. I need time to work what starts out as a conversation into a slight flirt. I need time to observe her and see if she is interested in me. I need time to observe and learn all I can about her so I can create a reason to exchange phone numbers with her on a non-flirt vector.

What I want to do with this HOT girl in this conversation is show her that I am 1) NOT some horny rude run-of-the mill guy only interested in women for sex; 2)That I might be interested in her; (I want her to suspect but not know for sure.) and 3) I want to give her a good non-flirt socially acceptable reason to give me her phone number.

Now let's go back to our original example. I am walking in the mall. I spot a hot woman approaching me and I simply approach her and say, "Excuse me, but I noticed what a sharp dresser you are and.(I continue with my story).I'm observing all the while if she is responding to me (trying to create the conversation with me too) or just answering my questions and trying to get out of there.

(I've learned a long time ago that there are a lot of wrong things that you can say to a girl, but once you stay clear of those, it doesn't matter much what you say. If a girl is responding to you, she will keep the conversation going. If she is not responding to you after a few moments of time, then she is married, in a relationship, or just not interested. I let those go and move on.

If you are in a place with a lot of women, it is a lot easier to qualify and move on quickly, then to beat one over the head with stupid conversation who is not interested.)

If I observe she is responding to me, I have a potential relationship (if I do it right.) I do not want to browbeat her with conversation either. I want to get in and get her phone number as smooth and as quick as possible. So I will talk just enough to find an in.

An "In" might be something like the following:

1) The girl says, "Thank you." when I compliment her taste, and then it comes out in the conversation she is a fashion consultant. I might then ask her if she consults men, and if she says she does, I will politely ask her for her card and say, “I've been wanting to do something like that. You know get a woman's viewpoint on how I should dress.”

2) Or it might come out in the conversation that she is a fashion model. Well I am an amateur photographer and I own several businesses, so I might say something like "You are! How much do you charge, because you would be totally perfect for this one project we are doing. Again, this will lead to an exchange of number and a future meeting.

3) Or if the woman really starts to flirt with me and shows a lot of interest, the conversation might go a little longer and head off into all kinds of mutually agreeable directions. There might be a topic that we were both really into, but I will usually end it before she does and say something like "Wow, you are really cool. I have to go right now. But I'd love to talk to you some more about that. In fact, I have some information that I know you'll just love. Let's trade numbers and I'll give you a call in a few days."

Now if you have followed me here. I've stopped the girl dead in her tracks. I've engaged her in a conversation that is NOT sex-oriented and "Hey what a HOT babe you are” oriented. And I've found some sort of mutual interest reason for us to meet again in the future. Last but not least, I've gotten her phone number.

If you do this right, it works about 90% of the time.

You have also undermined the reasons why a HOT girl would never have a relationship with some guy who hits up on her on the street. You did not hit up on her. She might have the impression (correctly) that you are interested in her, but she does not know for sure. By the time that you meet her and do start gradiently to hit up on her, you are not some guy on the street. You are a guy she already knows.

Now there is one more tough situation to handle. You are driving down the street in your car and you see a hot woman walking down the street. Actually, this is even a little harder than a woman walking down the street or in the mall.

Basically, you have to be in the right position and on the right street. It is not something you can usually cruise around and create. It is just something that you have to be ready to take advantage of if the right circumstances arise.

Have you ever had anyone say excuse me from a car while you were a pedestrian and ask you for directions? Well the approach is something like that, except you use one of your pre-thought out approaches rather than asking for directions which again is not a conversation but a question and answer.

Your pre-thought out approach might be something like:

1) "Excuse me, but could you help me for a minute." After they approach your car to hear what you have to say. "I really couldn't help but notice your style. I really like the way you are dressed. Do you do fashion consulting by any chance, because my sister or cousin really needs a makeover and your style would just be perfect for them."

2) Or if they were getting into their car. "Excuse me, but I noticed you have a Honda Civic. Are they really as good as they say? I was thinking of getting one."

Once you get past the point that you are in a car and they are on the street, everything else is pretty much the same.

Meeting Women in Stores, Restaurants, Malls, etc.

OK , so let's go on to Situation 2 - Approaching a woman who is stationary in a store, in a mall, a restaurant, etc.

Now, there are two kinds of stationary. 1) A woman can be standing in the clothes section of a store looking at some shirts, which gives you a relatively short period of time to act, or 2) she could be sitting at the table next to yours in a restaurant while you are eating. This gives you a much longer period of time to act.

Now the first situation is usually one in which the woman is not looking to meet anyone. She is shopping at the Gap or the grocery store and has other things on her mind. You only have a matter of seconds to pull it off. And she may be married or in a serious relationship and not interested

This is a situation in which I again would never use out-and-out flirt techniques, unless the woman flirts with me first. Remember, hot women don't think much of men who flirt with them on the street. It is obvious to them that the only reason the guy is approaching them is because of their looks, because the guy obviously doesn't know anything else about them.

(Conversely, if a girl is Not so hot, or even HOT but insecure, she would be much more open to flirting leading to a serious relationship because she doesn't get guys hitting on her AT ALL for her looks.)

What I use in this situation is usually the gradient no-flirt technique. Usually I have to mentally prepare for this depending on where I am. I have a series of questions thought out ahead of time that I can ask a woman in a situation, that are situationally and socially acceptable.

So say I am in the mall, for example. I am shopping in Macy's and I see this real hot woman looking at shoes in the Woman's shoes department. Now before hand, I have thought out several strategies that I can approach her with, like (I gave these two you before, but let's refresh your memory):

1) Her clothes - My buddy had to go out of town on an emergency and asked me to pick up something for this new girl he is dating. She loves clothes. I notice that you a sharp dresser. I like your style. I have good taste, but I have no clue where to buy clothes like that. Where would you suggest I go shopping around here.

Again this will not be perceived as a flirt, but a cry for help by the woman I approach. At the same time, I DO compliment her and make her feel good about her personality because I am basically saying I like her style and think she dresses well. Another factor that is good about this approach is it creates time - a conversation rather than a quick answer. It is a lot better than approaching a woman and saying "Do you know where BEBE is?"

Also notice that I make it known I am shopping for my Buddy's girlfriend which gives her the impression that I may be single and also subtly lets her know that I am NOT a slime ball cheating on my own girlfriend. (If she eventually perceives I am flirting with her.)

2) Her smell - Again I am shopping for my friend who is out of town on an emergency or for my Mom (easier to do this with perfume than clothes) and I notice, she had a nice smelling perfume on. What is it? Where can I get it? She obviously has good taste in perfumes. Are there any other perfumes she would recommend?

3) If all else fails and I can't think of anything. I will fall back on an old standby. I will ask if she knows what time it is. This is much harder because it is not a conversation. It is a question and answer. It only creates a few seconds of interaction. So the second part of this is to notice something about her in the three seconds that you have while she is giving you the time. Like "Wow" what a cool watch. Where did you get that?" Or "Wow, those are really neat shoes." Or "What cool earrings?"

Now the point of all these strategies is to get into communication with the woman on a non-flirting vector. She sees me as a guy just looking for some help. This is VERY important because now the HOT woman WILL consider me a prospect for a relationship even though she met me on the street, because I am NOT some random guy just hitting up on her for her looks.

The point of creating a conversation is twofold. It creates TIME. I need time to work what starts out as a conversation into a slight flirt. I need time to observe her and see if she is interested in me. I need time to observe and learn all I can about her so I can create a reason to exchange phone numbers with her on a non-flirt vector.

What I want to do with this HOT girl in this conversation is show her that I am 1) NOT some horny rude run-of-the mill guy only interested in women for sex; 2). That I might be interested in her (I want her to suspect but not know for sure.) and 3) give her a good non-flirt socially acceptable reason to give me her phone number.

Now let's go back to our original example. I am walking in the mall. I spot a hot woman shopping in the woman's shoe section. Now the approach is VERY important. You have to move quickly, if you hang around and look at her waiting for the best time, you start to look like a pervert-stalker and even start feeling like one after awhile.

So as soon as you see her you start to move in for the kill. The best position to start a conversation from is sort of shoulder to shoulder, next to her with your attention on clothes or shoes, while she is looking at the same. However, you have to be prepared for her to move at any time. You don't know what she is going to do. Once you commit you can't back down if the position is not right (unless she is walking away from you with her back towards you -the you can sort of meander after her until you get in position again without looking like a stalker.)

If she suddenly turns and starts walking at you, however, be prepared to shift gears and treat it like "How To Pick Up a Girl Walking Down The Street".

Now if everything goes right and she is not moving but just looking at shoes, realize that this situation is slightly different from the girl walking down the street because unlike the girl walking down the street she is focused on buying shoes, and her attention may be a little further away. She may need a little more time to respond to you.

So we start off on a lower gradient. Notice what she is putting her attention on, and casually ask her a question about that while you are standing next to her looking away from her (looking at some shoes yourself.)

So the lower gradient might begin with you saying something like. "Do you know if that brand is very comfortable?" She will respond to you with some polite answer, but it will also give her time for her attention to transist from what she is looking at to you.

During this transition time, you can turn your head slightly and look at her as she talks to you. If she is not looking at you when she talks but continues to look at the clothes, then continue at this gradient not really looking at her, but talking about what she has her attention on until she finally turns and looks at you.

When she turns and looks at you, turn your head and look at her. Now that you got her attention, sort of make a head or face gesture like you just noticed something about her and say something like "You know, I just noticed what a sharp dresser you are and.(Continue with your pre-thought-out story. Observing all the while if she is responding to you - trying to create the conversation with you too, or just answering your questions and trying to get out of there.)

If I observe she is responding to me, I have a potential relationship (if I do it right.) I do not want to browbeat her with conversation either. I want to get in and get her phone number as smooth and as quick as possible. So I will talk just enough to find an in.

An "In" might be something like the following:

1) The girl says, "Thank you." when I compliment her taste, and then it comes out in the conversation she is a fashion consultant. I might then ask her if she consults men, and if she says she does, I will politely ask her for her card and say I've been wanting to do something like that. You know get a woman's viewpoint on how I should dress.

2) Or it might come out in the conversation that she is a fashion model. Well I am an amateur photographer and I own several businesses, so I might say something like "You are! How much do you charge, because you would be totally perfect for this one project we are doing. Again, this will lead to an exchange of number and a future meeting.

3) Or if the woman really starts to flirt with me and shows a lot of interest, the conversation might go a little longer and head off into all kinds of mutually agreeable directions. There might be a topic that we were both really into, but I will usually end it before she does and say something like "Wow, you are really cool. I have to go right now. But I'd love to talk to you some more about that. In fact, I have some information that I know you'll just love. Let's trade numbers and I'll give you a call in a few days."

Now if you have followed me here. I've gotten into non-sexual oriented conversation with the girl by talking about whatever she had her attention on, got her attention off of that and onto me. I've continued to engage her in a conversation that is NOT sex oriented and "Hey what a HOT babe you are, oriented." And I've found some sort of mutual interest reason for us to meet again in the future. Last but not least, I've gotten her phone number.

If you do this right, it works about 90% of the time.

You have also undermined the reasons why a HOT girl would never have a relationship with some guy who hits up on her on the street. You didn't hit up on her. She might have the impression (correctly) that you are interested in her, but she doesn't know for sure. By the time that you meet her and do start gradiently to hit up on her, you are not some guy on the street. You are a guy she already knows.

Now when a woman is sitting next to you in a restaurant, in a theatre, at a bar where she is close enough that you can hear her conversation, there can be a slightly different situation and approach. If she is alone, it is pretty much the same. Notice what she is putting her attention on and start talking about that.

However, if she is with a friend, or talking on a cell phone, if you can hear her conversation or see her personality from her motions and how she acts with this other person. Rather than using a pre-thought-out approach, you are going to use what you learn from observing and listening to her to create an approach on the spot.

So by listening to her, for example, you may find out she is an interior decorator. Well rather than saying "Excuse me I couldn't help but notice how fashionably you dress. You will say something like "Excuse me but I couldn't help but hear that you are an interior decorator. I am looking for someone to give me an estimate on a few things to redo my apartment. You seem very creative and intelligent. Do you have a card? "

If you get the right ammunition, this will work 100% of the time.

What do you do with these women when you meet them for the future meeting?

Well, it helps if you think out your strategies so that it is not totally a lie or arbitrary. You meet them for the express purpose that you agreed upon, but you show interest, qualify them (probe to find out if they are married, etc.) and as long as the person is showing interest in you, you gradiently flirt a little and take it to the next level when you feel it is right. If the person is definitely NOT showing interest in you and is all business, you end your meeting as soon as you can and never call them back.

Sometimes, rather than waste my time in a meeting I am unsure about I will qualify the woman over the phone.

When I call her I will confess, for example, that I really did not need a interior decorator, that I just really liked her personality from what I could overhear. She was there with her girlfriend and I did not want to intrude on her dinner meeting, so I asked for her card just so I could get a chance to talk to her and check her out.

Or if the interior decorator thing was truly an interest of mine. I may talk about that for awhile try to flirt a little then say that I DO need an interior decorator but that wasn't my only motive for asking her for her card. Then I will tell her I really liked her personality and ask her if she is married or living with someone?

I've never had anyone get mad at me when I put it that way, and you will find out real quick if there is any interest.

I still keep these first conversations and meetings on a light flirt. I never talk about how beautiful they are, but only compliment them about their personality or personality qualities. (e.g. I like their style. I like their taste. They seem very creative, intelligent, etc.)

Remember you met these hot girls on the street (so to speak), and the only way to get over their tendency not to have a real relationship with a guy they met on the street, is to really let them see that you like them for qualities other than their physical beauty. I usually will not let a hot girl know how hot I really think she is until after we have started sexual activity like making-out or petting, etc.

In the second section of this Chapter "Meeting Women Walking Down the Street" I gave you a techniques for the hardest situations of all - meeting a woman while she is moving and meeting a woman while she is walking and you are in a car.

In this section, we talked about approaching a woman who is stationery in a store, library, grocery store, etc. In the next section "Meeting Women Who Work In Malls, Restaurants, Stores, etc." we will talk about the final condition. -- Approaching a woman who works in a store, mall, etc. and who will be there again and again.

Meeting Women Who Work in Malls, Restaurants, Stores, etc.

Meeting women who work in stores is a little easier than the prior situations. As when a woman works in a store, restaurant, or library, you have more time available to you. You don't have 3 seconds to make a move as you sometimes do when a woman is walking towards you in a mall.

Because a woman has a job and you know where she works, you can make a long term plan to develop a relationship with her and she will not see it the same as some guy who says, "Hey Baby" three seconds after he first sees her.

When we are talking about approaching a woman who works in a store, or restaurant, etc. and who will be there again unlike the other "street meeting strategies" you can be an out-and-out flirt or take the gradient no-flirt technique. Both techniques can work in this situation.

Let's take out-and out flirting first. How do you apply that? Remember, hot women do not think much of men who flirt with them on the street because it is obvious to them that the only reason the guy is approaching them is because of their looks, because the guy obviously doesn't know anything else about them. That is less of a concern here, but it still applies to a degree.

Hot women get hit up on all the time. You have to be different from all the other guys. So we never come out and say that we actually think they are hot. We just let them know we are interested and create a little mystery out of exactly "how" interested we are. When we compliment physical qualities, we say things like "You have pretty eyes." "You have nice lips!" "I like your style" "You dress so well." "I like your earrings." Get it.

Statements like these let a woman know we are interested without being like all the other guys who tell them they are "Soooo beautiful" "So Hot" "So fine" repeatedly over and over again in the first ten minutes that they meet them.

We qualify. We ask questions. We talk about interests and personality attributes. We DO NOT repeat physical compliments. We say "You have pretty eyes" once and never bring it up again until AFTER we are having a sexual relationship with them. We don't give many physical compliments at all. But the compliments we do give and repeat are "I like your energy!" "I like your style!" "You are so smart!" And so forth.

We come and we go and we never overstay our welcome. We want the girl to ask us to stay longer.

This way a woman gets to know you and considers that you are getting to know her and that you like her for her personality not just her looks.

This way she will fall in love with you.

© 2007 Dating To Relating, Inc

How do I flirt on that first meeting?

Well sometimes, I simply let them wait on me while I'm shopping. I'll smile, be pleasant, and ask them how their day is going. This show them, interest and creates mystery. They do not know if I am really interested or just friendly. At some point, I may tell them they have pretty eyes or a great smile or a great tan, etc. Something to let them know I'm flirting. If they withdraw and get cold all of a sudden, then they probably are married, have a boyfriend, or just are not interested. I let it go because there are hundreds of other girls in the mall or other shops.

When I am in a busy shop with lots of people I usually do the above. When I see a pretty girl all alone is a shop by herself with no customers. I will be much more aggressive as the situation is more lax. (No customers, no boss, - a lot less distractions. She is usually bored and riper for flirting.)

A line that I use that ALWAYS gets a friendly chuckle is to be very overt about the flirting. I usually walk up to them with a nice smile and say, "It's pretty slow in here. Are you doing OK or do you need someone to flirt with you?"

Like I said, I always get a friendly chuckle with that one. But if the girl is married or something they will tell me, or if they are not interested in me they will side step the question and just talk about how slow it is. If they are interested, they will come back with a flirt themselves. Something like, "Well a girl can always use a flirt."

So we keep flirting to a light gradient and we keep from scaring the woman by withdrawing and not being obsessive. Now the gradient of flirt and the frequency of calling back on her can vary depending on how heavily she flirts back with you. With some women, you can set a date in just one flirtatious meeting. Others take months of calling back on them like once a week or so.

Even with the gradient no-flirt technique, if the girl is responsive you begin to flirt on the second or third visit.

Girls who work in stores or restaurants can be easy picking, if you do it right. There are even special types of jobs that are especially responsive to the no flirt technique.

I use to love to get massages (legitimate) and went to massage parlors frequently as a young man. It was easy for me to pick up on these types of girls because practically every guy that came through these hotels and other legitimate massage places was still a pervert.

When I could let them massage me naked and still not get overtly turned on (I learned how to control myself very quickly), and flirt with them non-sexually and tell them what a nice personality they had. I would score real big. Real quick. I would be like the first non-pervert they had seen in months and if I would return and ask them out on a date, they ALWAYS would say OK.

So when a girl has a job and you know where and when she works, it is pretty easy to establish a relationship with her. Just take your time, get to know her and keep the flirting light if she is really HOT.

How and Where to Meet Women

A lot of guys ask me where is the best place to find girls, to find dates?

The answer is that once you are skilled, it is anywhere, anytime, any place.

But for those who aren't quite that skilled and for those who are very particular and are looking for a certain kind of girl, a certain age of girl, a certain type of girl, etc. this question takes on much more importance.

I use to think (like a lot of guys do) that finding dates was the hardest thing in the world to do, but after having gone on 700 dates in one year, I now think it is one of the easier things to do. The harder question to answer, I believe, is how do you find the right girl for you?

But the question before us now is how and where to find dates, So the following are some good places to meet women.

On the Street - Meeting women that you can actually see has its advantages over internet and classified meetings. Thus, meeting women on the street. - stores, malls, parks, concerts, events, the beach, grocery stores, Starbucks, etc. - allows you to see the real deal. You can see what they look like without being victim to the 10-year-old pictures that you find on the internet, and you can see what their personality is like without it being disguised by internet dribble-drabble.

It is one of my favorite ways to meet women but it is something I have to do when I have a lot of time because pound for pound meeting women on the street successfully is much more time intensive then internet and classified advertising. (And by successfully, I don't mean just getting a phone number. Lots of guys can do that to no avail. I mean turning a meeting on the street into a girlfriend, a lover, a relationship!)

It can also be one of the hardest ways to successfully meet women, depending on the situation. Ninety-nine percent of the hot women that I have dated have told me they would never go out with a guy who approaches them on the street no matter how good looking and cool he was.

Stopping a woman on the street who is walking is also extremely hard to do successfully. However, meeting women who work in restaurants, book stores, malls, etc. can be an extremely easy way to meet women as you know where they work and you can come back to see them repeatedly to check them out.

If you seriously want to be a skilled craftsman at meeting women, meeting them on the street is something you definitely have to master. Once you master it, the above datum - anytime, anywhere, any place - will be real to you.

Bars and Clubs - I don't recommend meeting women in bars and clubs if you are looking for a sane relationship. If you just want a one-night stand then bars and clubs can be easy pickings. If you are interested in this kind of stuff, you should read Chapter 2(c) above.

Clubs and social groups - Now this is probably one of the better ways to meet women. It has a couple of advantages built in. By choosing the right club or group, you can pre-qualify a woman on interests and compatibility.

Think smart! - When joining clubs or other social activities to find and meet women, remember this - chose a club or group or activity that is more likely to have the characteristics that are important to you. If you like "hot women" get involved with a modeling agency or acting lessons. If you like smart women, take a class at a community college or join a chess club or MENSA.

Also another smart thing to do is to try to join groups in which most of the participants are women. I went on a job interview when I was about 25 for a job as an airline steward. Back then, men were rare. I remember it well. There were about 50 hot girls in the room and ME. No other guys. Girls get very competitive in these situations; I had at least three of the girls hitting up on me the whole time without me doing a thing.

So you might want to consider taking crochet lessons or the one they use in the movies all the time - ballet!

Dating Clubs and Dating counselors - I have used dating clubs, dating services, and dating counselors – the services that give you personal handpicked dates. In general, I find them rather expensive compared to the internet. Perhaps equally effective, but just a lot more expensive. It really depends on the service. Ask to see some pictures and communicate what you are looking for. Try to get some guarantees as the salesman will tell you anything to get a sale.

Speed Dating - This can be a fairly good way to meet people. It is quick and to the point. Like dating clubs, it depends on the membership and who is sponsoring it. But whenever you can meet a lot of people quickly it is a good idea as it is both cost and time effective.

Friends - Working your friends and even associates for leads can be very worthwhile. It is free and usually doesn't take long. Most of the leads I have gotten this way have been superior to internet, classifieds, and dating clubs. Since it is free, it is certainly worth giving it a shot. Just tell your friends what you are looking for and ask them if they know anyone who is single and would possibly be interested.

On line dating sites - for people on the go and who have a busy life style, Internet dating has certain advantages. The main one being that you can check out tons of people in a short period of time. The quality factor I find to be low with internet dating, however, as most people tend to present their best side by exaggerating or lying about their personality, their age, and their looks. This is especially true for the over 35 crowd.

Internet dating works better for some people than others. Once you get internet dating down, however, it can be a source of unlimited dates. It is part of the strategy I used to get 700 dates in a year and continue to use to meet as many women as I want with little effort.

On line and off line classified and personal ads - Classified ads whether on or off line is equal to or better than on line dating sites as a way to meet women. However, again it depends on the service you subscribe to. I have personally done better with both the number of leads and the quality of leads that I get from classified advertising than online dating sites. I have also done worse. It is part of the strategy I used to get 700 dates in one year. If you are interested in this area, you should read my eBook "How I Got 700 Dates in One Year" for a more detailed treatise on how to use classified advertising and online dating sites to generate unlimited dates.

Social community sites - MySpace.com and all the new community sites also offer a source of free internet dating. You can check out people's profiles and place classified ads, etc. Again, I find placing the classified ads to work better than contacting profiles as MySpace in particular is so full of spam profiles that it has almost become a waste of time to contact people in terms of effort and return on effort.

If you want to contact profiles, joining a group is usually a good idea. That way you can meet people with similar interests. Joining group and contacting group members and placing classified ads tends to reduce the effort and weed out the spam profile responses. Doing a profile search on MySpace and contacting the hot women is not a good idea for they are almost ALL spam profiles trying to sell you something or other.

If you still want to contact profiles, then you had better learn how to differentiate the spam profiles from real girls and only bother contacting the real girls.

MySpace is also geared towards a younger teenage mentality and is not really a singles dating service, so contacting women on there is not quite the same as contacting a bunch of women on Match.com

All in all it can work for some people. And if you learn how to approach it right, it can be very workable indeed. But in general, If I am going to put time into internet dating sites, I'd rather work Match.com than MySpace.

In summary

Personally, when I want quality dates, I work the street. When I want quantity of dates, I work the internet and classified advertising sites. I find these to be the best strategies overall.

7) TURNING DATING INTO RELATIONSHIPS

How to Get a Second Date With a Woman

Ninety percent of the women I go out with on a first date (and most of these are blind dates), want to have a sexual relationship with me by the end of the date. So guys have asked me, "What is the biggest mistake guys make on the first date that prevents ever having a second date or developing a sexual relationship (rather than a friendship)?"

Well there are several mistakes a guy can make. Let me summarize them here then go into more detail. MISTAKES ARE:

1) Talking about yourself too much. Trying to be interesting instead of INTERESTED

2) NOT ASKING QUESTIONS AND NOT LISTENING ENOUGH.

3) FOCUSING TOO MUCH ON SEX-- either overtly or by innuendo.

4) NOT USING SUBTLETIES ENOUGH (What a woman understands)

5) NOT DEVELOPING SEXUAL FLOW OR INTEREST.

6) NOT CREATING FUTURE. (A relationship is ALL about FUTURE.)

The first mistake that most guys make is that they go on the first date and talk all about themselves, sort of strut around telling the girl that he's got this car, and he's got this job and he talks and talks and talks bragging about this and that trying to impress the girl that he is a good catch.

What a girl sees is a self-centered egomaniac that isn't going to be able to take care of her at all, because he is not interested in her and doesn't listen to what she has to say. Not a good relationship prospect.

Another way of saying it is that guys try to be interesting. They figure they have to be interesting for a girl to be interested in them. Sorry guys, but it doesn't work that way.

You have to be INTERESTED in the girl, not INTERESTING to get her attention. Did you ever see two interesting people on a date. It is hilarious! They are both so busy trying to be interesting to the other that neither has time to be interested in the other.

If you don't know what I am talking about, think what makes you feel better. A girl who is INTERESTED in you? Or a girl who is telling you how cool she is, how hot she is, etc. and all kinds of other INTERESTING things?

INTERESTING leads to a lot of rejection and "platonic" friendships by the way. Girls will be friends with a guy who is really interesting. Why? Girls like to be amused and entertained. Interesting men are sort of like children to them. A source of non-sexual amusement and pleasure.

Then there are the guys who are SCARED S***less and don't know what to say. So they say all kinds of useless and banal and irrelevant stuff to again be INTERESTING to the girl.

Then there are guys who dread silence. So whenever there is a silent moment they feel awkward and have to fill the silence with some noise, so they open their mouths and say something trite and banal again just to keep the conversation going and again to be INTERESTING to the girl. - THEY AREN'T. You don't have to fill silence with verbal chatter. Maybe it is a good time for some non-verbal communication -- like a smile, or a light touch.

90% of the girls I have a first date with want to go out with me again and have a relationship with me. WHY? Well, the biggest factor is I am INTERESTED in getting to know them. So I never come scripted, I am always just there and I ask questions designed to get to know the person in front of me. THE SECRET: Well, I just said part of it, so here is it all.

I AM INTERESTED. I ASK QUESTIONS and then I LISTEN TO THE ANSWERS. Based on the answer they give, I may ask another question or I might say something that I know they would be interested in knowing because of what they just said. MOST of the time I spend about 80% of my time on a date LISTENING. Girls like that.

ANOTHER BIG MISTAKE GUYS MAKE that prevents a second date is putting too much conversation attention on sex, sexual topics, sexual innuendos, and her looks.

ALL WOMEN THINK that ALL GUYS JUST WANT SEX. So basically, they are right and guys have to realize that girls have our number and are not impressed by it. GIRLS already KNOW you want sex. She wouldn't even be there on the first date, if she weren't vaguely OK with the concept of having sex with you. What she wants to know is: What ELSE do you want? What ELSE do you like about her? What ELSE can you do for her? What ELSE do you have in common with her? How ELSE can you have fun together?

So, LISTEN to what she talks about, because if you listen you will get clues.

GIRLS communicate in SUBTLETIES and like to be communicated to with SUBTLETIES.

As a rule, I NEVER tell a good-looking woman she is good looking until the 3rd or 4th date. That is a subtle communication that tells her that I am not like all the other guys who kiss her behind.

So, you see, you don't have to tell a woman how pretty she is on a first date. (Especially if she is gorgeous, because she gets so much of this so often, it actually becomes a turn-off to her.) You can complement her on her dress, or her shoes, or you can say she has a nice personality (find something non-sexual you like about her and complement it) or you could say but only once and non-repetitively) she has pretty eyes, or a cute nose, or a nice smile, or she has pretty hands. (Always pick a non-sexual part of the body to complement)

So if you don't talk about yourself and sex, what DO you talk about? Talk about whatever the girl wants to talk about. LISTEN, and base your conversation off of what she is interested in. Ask questions about her. BUT you should have two goals for the night....

1) DEVELOPING SEXUAL FLOW OR INTEREST.

Now you don't want to TALK about SEXUAL stuff too much, but that does not mean you don't want to get the old sexual juices going. BUT you do that mostly non-verbally, not verbally (Unless she starts a sexual conversation with you.) Now some of the DATING GURUS have rea good courses on how a man can be sexy and get a woman's attention sexually. (David DeAngelo's course comes to mind.) And this is an in depth topic deserving of its own book. So let's just say it is done with posture, manners, attitude, movement, voice rhythms, and the occasional moving in close and the withdrawing, or light touch or holding ofthe hand momentarily. Verbally is done with the right gradient of topic. If you do it right, the woman will always give you a goodnight kiss as a further way of testing that sector out, and let you know by her non-verbal signals, whether you should continue or just let it go with a simple light kiss. It is better to develop it, make the woman want more, and walk away than to over reach and destroy everything else you have built up here. A simple hug, or a light kiss on the cheek or the mouth is what I do on 90% of my first dates that I am interested in.

2)CREATE FUTURE

What is future? Well if you are going to have a relationship with someone, rather than just a one-date-goodbye. You have to have some future interaction. AND FUTURE IS NOT "Can we go out again sometime?" That is definitely NOT FUTURE. That is a plea! Begging! And this will definitely scare them away. (Watch "Blind Date" on TV some time.)

Future is scheduling something that you both would be interested in doing for whatever reasons, sometime in the future--something with value to both of you. YOU may want to have SEX with the girl right away in the future. BUT SHE DOESN'T- not yet. She wants to get to know you a little better. So FUTURE is a way that she can get to know you a little better, before deciding if she wants to have a sexual relationship with you or not. GIRLS LIKE THAT. And girls like guys who understand that.

YOU SEE the girl wouldn't go out on the first date with you if there weren't some possibility that she could have sex with you.

(BEING THERE is a subtle communication. She wouldn't be there if she wasn't somewhat interested.) So, unless you blow it, you will get sex eventually. HOWEVER, most guys DO blow it 9 out of 10 times instead of closing as I do 9 out of 10 times. So how to create FUTURE? Well on a date it is relatively easy. APPLY what I have said above. ASK QUESTIONS and LISTEN. She will tell you something that gives you a subtle opportunity to see her again, and it should be something she would be really interested in and it won't scare her off.

EXAMPLE OF WHAT WORKS:

While you are listening, she talks about the math class she is taking in college she is having trouble with.You happen to me a math genius. You simply say, "Well I am really good at math. If you would like some help with your homework. Let me know." Then shut up. If she is interested in you, she will take the bait and say. "Yeah, oh I would so appreciate that" or something of the sort. If you have totally blown it by now and she doesn't want your help despite her learning disability, she won't take the bait. THAT WON'T HAPPEN unless you violated something else I have talked about here, and you talked about yourself too much, tried to be interesting, didn't listen, talked about sex or how pretty she was too much.

Another example is, while you are listening she says how she really likes to go dancing. So if you like dancing you say, "Really, me too. I love dancing, let's do that sometime." Or if you don't like to dance, don't lie. Say, "Really, then maybe you could help me because I don't know a thing about dancing but I think it’s time I learned. Do you think you could teach me a little sometime?”

GET IT. Come up with something you guys could do in the future that she and you would really like to do, that's not a plea "Can we go out again?"

How to Turn the Second, Third and Fourth Dates into a Girlfriend

There are a lot of guys that I meet that can get a first date and even a second, third and fourth date without ever turning that situation into a girlfriend. Or they meet with her a few times then she dumps them.

If I get a second date with a girl there is about a 99.9% certainty that she will be my girlfriend if I want her to. It is totally up to me.

So if you don't blow it on that first date what do you do on the second date? The third date? The fourth date?

It can go further that that if you are really interested in a relationship. There are plenty of women that take 10 to 15 dates to really establish a sexual relationship with. So what do you do on dates two through fifteen or to put it another way on those series of dates where you are meeting a woman but you have not yet established a sexual relationship with her.

Now some girls will have sex with a guy on the first date. Others it takes more like three dates. Usually it depends on their moral code, and sometimes the older and more experienced a woman gets with respect to men, the longer she will take to check men out. Consequently, some women take 10 to 15 dates before they have sex with a guy. Now, it is not as if you do not mess around with these girls at all. They just will not go all the way, until they are sure about you. I have gone out with many girls on a weekly basis that took three months before we had intercourse.

Yes, I know it sounds a little odd coming from me. After all, if you have been following my writings, you know that I am also the guy who picked up women in a bar or club and had sex with then in the back seat of my car in the parking lot and then went back into the club looking for more.

But that is and was a different situation. I was not looking for a relationship when I did those kinds of things. I was just looking to get laid. And I did - night after night after night.

When you are looking for a girlfriend, immediate sexual gratification is not the most important thing to be looking for. Sex is part of a good boyfriend/girlfriend relationship but compatibility, personality, communication, and respect are issues that are by far more important.

Girls know that. That is why most of them won't enter into a quick sexual relationship with a guy they are considering for a boyfriend. They want to check him out first and make sure he has acceptable qualities. Some women take longer to check you out than others. Hence, some will sleep with you after a few dates while others it takes a few months.

If you do the wrong things during this dating "check out" stage, then they will never sleep with you. They might not even kiss you during those first dates....Horrors!

If you have gotten past that all important first date and the girl agrees to go out with you again, then plain and simple she is interested in you and you have a chance at a relationship - provided you don't blow it from that point on.

So what do you do during this "check out" stage to end up with a girlfriend? How do you not "blow it?" Well the easiest way to answer that question is that you do the same thing that they do. Check them out and see if you really want to get involved with them or not. And most importantly communicate that that is what you are doing to them while you are doing it.

Listen to a woman. Check her out. Ask her questions. Women love to talk. They'll tell you everything you need to know if you just listen and ask questions. The mistake is to focus on sex and start telling her things to impress her, so she will want to have sex with you.

Qualify the woman. Do you really like her? Do you want to spend time with her? What would she be like if you did spend 24/7 with her?

If you really do like a woman and you qualify her by asking questions to get to know her better every time you see her, she will love you for it. Why? Because, she will know that you are really interested in her. That it is NOT just about sex for you. That you have values. And if you are compatible it will be obvious to both of you as you ask questions back and forth.

Develop your own philosophy on dating. Communicate it when it is appropriate. Then shut up and listen some more. You do have to talk. You do have to say things, but your talk is brief. It is asking questions, communicating your philosophy, and responding appropriately and honestly, when they ask you questions. But let the woman do most of the talking. Believe it or not, if you ask questions and listen to the answers you will be much more in control of the dates.

You should definitely have a philosophy worked out about dating and relationships before you start dating. Even if your philosophy is, "I have no clue. I just take it one day at a time." That is ok. It doesn't matter what your dating philosophy is. Just have one worked out. When she asks you questions give her answers that are consistent with your philosophy. If her behavior strays from your philosophy make it known that you are not interested in that.

I make my philosophy known right away on my first and subsequent dates. I gently repeat the theme throughout my early dating. What is my philosophy? I tell a woman the truth. That I am looking for a long-term relationship. I want to get married again and have more kids. I've been cheated on by women and don't like it. I believe in monogamy. But most importantly I think it takes a while to really get to know a person.

I'm not jealous or possessive. I'm totally ok with her seeing other guys and dating other guys while we are dating. I think that that is actually healthy and that I think a healthy relationship evolves like this. People meet and start dating with no restrictions on dating other people. Then one day a couple of weeks or months down the road, they turn to each other and ask each other if they are still seeing other people. They each say "No." When two people evolve monogamy naturally just because they want to, without any restrictive agreements. You have a good thing.

That is my philosophy and what I actually believe.

Now, as dates two through fifteen evolve. No matter what comes up, I repeat and refer back to my philosophy.

If a girl asks me on the second or third date (they usually don't) if I am seeing or having sex with anyone. I say yes and tell them the truth. Why? Because truth works. I tell them I don't know them well enough to be exclusive with them yet. That my sexual relationship(s) are not serious - just fun. That these relationships don't ultimately satisfy me because I am looking for the woman I can marry, have kids and a monogamous relationship with.

I also tell them that these relationships keep me sane. I am not horny, so I don't make stupid decisions and get with a potential girlfriend candidate just because I haven't had sex in a year. I have to like someone to get with them.

You see, no matter what a girl brings up or what happens it somehow fits into my philosophy and I communicate it. If after having sex with a woman - say after the third or fourth date or even three months of dating - if she says, "You don't seem really into me like most guys."

I tell her the truth. "I really like you, but how could I be INTO you when we have only gone out on three dates (or for three months). If you want this to go faster, then we need to spend more time together. Get to know each other better."

Get the idea?

Talk to the girl. Make your dating philosophy known and either you will blow her away because she is not compatible or you will end up with a good compatible girlfriend

What about making "the move"?

Well, you have to get physical with a woman if you want to turn dating into a relationship. So, do you make the move on the second date? Third date? Tenth date?

There is no answer to this. Each woman is different. But if you listen and observe, you will know when the time is right. Women will tell you or show you.

I've gone out with women who have overtly asked me to make out with them on the first date. I've gone out with women who have just had that "look" that told me I should kiss them - right now.

I've gone out with women that would only give me a hand shake on the first date. But when I asked them out for a second, a third, a fourth date, they always said yes. That tells me something. It tells me they are interested in me but just very conservative.

Usually with this kind of woman, by the third or fourth date, I start getting a little hug and a cheek kiss, but more importantly, the women usually start talking about sex and asking me how I like this or that sexually and sort of qualifying me on the subject of sex.

When they start talking about sex, this is a big clue. So the next date, I usually give them a choice. I say to these very polite and restrained women, "Would you like to go to dinner and a movie again or do you want to just hang out at home and relax, cuddle and watch some TV?"

You see, when they start talking about sex, I know despite their rather conservative behavior that they are ready for it. So, I give them a choice just to confirm my suspicions. When they chose to stay at home (and they always do), I know it is time to take it to the next level.

Date two through fifteen are all actually very similar. Some women will do on date fifteen what other women will do on date two. Some women just need more time to get comfortable with you. They need more gradients.

It is all about comfort. Some women feel they are intuitive and know in a few minutes after meeting you whether they can get along with you or not. These women will usually enter into a sexual relationship quickly.

Other women feel that it takes a long time to get to really know a man. So they proceed more cautiously. If you ask a woman questions about dating while you are getting to know her, she will usually reveal her own dating philosophy. Then you will know how to proceed.

Some women will even tell you that they want the guy to take charge and set the pace. Other women want to be in control and need respect from a guy. Some women want a guy to try even though they will constantly shut him down until they are ready. The fact that the guy tries makes them feel good and desired.

Other women don't like guys to try too much at all. They give you little signals and they want you to respect and respond to the signals they give. Other women like to be aggressive. Still others like shy guys.

There is no one right way for a guy to behave with a woman. If you use a strategy, you will only be right 10-30 percent of the time. If you simply talk to women, ask questions, and listen to the answers, they will tell you where they are at about things and what to do to get them. If you approach it this way, you can be right 70-90 percent of the time.

I close about 90 percent of the women I meet on a first date for a second date. And when I get a second date, it is a done deal. A relationship is mine if I want it.

I have made plenty of mistakes over the years however. But usually the ones I lose are the oddball crazy ones. The ones that don't fit any pattern that I have seen before, but are none-the-less crazy.

For example, I have lost women on dates 2 - 5 by not being sexually aggressive enough. This usually happened when women were giving me mixed signals. Telling me either verbally or with body language that they didn't want to have sex yet, then ending things later complaining that I wasn't aggressive enough.

I have also lost women on dates 2-5 by being too aloof. Usually hot women like it when I am aloof and not chasing after them. I never, never, never tell a woman she is "Hot" on the first date or even for a few dates after that. I might only begin to tell her after we are having sex, how hot I think she is. But occasionally you get a woman who is "hot" with very low self esteem and she needs that attention from guys that most hot women hate. I lose them because they are not confident enough in themselves to chase after me.

Losing the crazy ones is not a big deal to me, however. In fact, I prefer it.

But, if you are a little crazy yourself, you might like that type of girl. So when you get mixed signals or suspect that there may be some deeper insecurity issues or low self-esteem going on with a girl that she is not revealing, be a little more observant. Expect the unexpected.

If I had been a little more observant, I probably would not have lost the crazy ones either.

And finally, remember your sex gradients. I've talked about them before.

Remember that "Negative Sex talk" (I don't like it when guys do this and guys do that" "You can't have sex with me, yet," etc.) is the first gradient of sexual interest. Positive sex talk is the next gradient.

The physical contact gradients come after those. Light touches with the hands while talking, bumping into each other slightly while walking, holding hands, kissing, making out, petting, heavy petting, intercourse.

So when a girl is not touching you or kissing you, don't necessarily give up on her. Talk to her. If she brings up "negative sex talk" or “positive sex talk" on her own, she is interested in you. But don't you be the one to bring it up or she might go into "Negative sex talk" as a reaction not as a flirt. Listen to her and see what she originates. Once she brings it up either positive or negative, join in.

8) RELATIONSHIPS - THE DIFFERENT TYPES OF SEXUAL RELATIONSHIPS

When we talk about relationships, and relating to women, the first thing you need to clear up is what kind of relationship are we talking about? There is a variety of types of relationships - friendship, familial, economic, and of course sexual.

In this Chapter, we are going to limit ourselves to talking about sexual relationships.

The major types of sexual relationships are:

Platonic
Prostitution
One Night Stands
Friends with Privileges
Dating with Casual Sex
Lovers Only
Arrangements
Multiple Lovers
Swinging
Open Relationships
Affairs
Girlfriend/Boyfriend
Living Together
Marriage

Attraction Vectors involved in Sexual Relationships

Sexual attraction - Sexual attraction can be a mutual sex attraction, or a one way sexual attraction with another dynamic attraction factor (money, emotion, power, status, political, mental stimulation, etc.) replacing or in addition to sexual attraction on the other's part.

Economic Attraction - We all know how this works - sex for money. Can be anything from prostitution to marriage. This vector can be very attractive to certain people. And can be an added attraction for others who thought they would never marry for money, so to speak, they certainly won't turn it down if everything else they are looking for is there.

Economic plus - This is a multi-vectored attraction that has money as a critical or qualifying attraction, but is not solely determined by the money factor alone. This category of relationship moves away from traditional prostitution's attraction to money.

Traditional prostitution is simple. A prostitute will have sex with ANYBODY who has money. A woman who only has sex with men she is sexually attracted to for money, might not be considered a prostitute - depending on how selective she is and how she goes about getting men to pay her.

A woman who would only get involved with a boyfriend who she is attracted to AND who has money enough to take care of her, would usually NOT be considered a prostitute. (But perhaps we would consider her a gold digger.)

Horny Attraction - many times people will get involved in a relationship solely because they are sexually needy or horny. Sometimes these will be brief "prostitution" or "one-night-stand" type relationships to get a little sexual relief now and again, other times they will be long term relationships to satisfy ongoing sexual needs while that person is looking for that "more than sex" partner. It is typical for one's standards to go down in a time when one is very needy.

Emotional Attraction - Emotional attraction can be either internal or mutual and is usually the most compelling factor in determining relationships for both men and women. (Although men are attracted to women for other factors (usually physical) emotional factors tend to be the deal clinchers.

Emotionally, we will often become attracted to a person who we know is REALLY attracted to us because we know they will be super nice to us and treat us right. Similarly, we are often attracted to people who make us feel cool, wanted, desirable, etc.

Whether this feeling is generated internally (the hot girl who does absolutely nothing for you but go out and look hot in front of all your friends thereby making you look cool and desirable to others) or externally (the not so hot girl who tells you over and over again how good looking, etc. you are), we all like relating to people who make us feel good about ourselves.

Other emotional attraction vectors influencing relationships involve friendship, compatibility, good communication, emotional support, and mental stimulation among others.

Companionship Attraction - Companionship is another vector that determines relationships. When we find good companions, we usually want to see them again and develop some sort of relationship with them. No one wants to be alone, when we find ourselves alone for whatever reason, we will usually seek out new relationships. If we don't have a lot of choices, we usually feel that anyone is better than no one and as a result we may end up with odd choices for friends at times to avoid being lonely.

Compatibility Attraction - Compatibility can be a powerful attraction from the beginning or it can sneak up on you as you slowly realize how compatible you are with someone.

Status Attraction - Many people are attracted to people with "high status" of one kind or another. It is another attraction vector that sort of acts like money. There are people who will actually "prostitute" themselves to be with someone of a "higher" status.

Power Attraction - Similar to status attraction many people are attracted to people with "power" of one kind or another. It is another attraction vector that sort of acts like money. Again, there are people who will actually "prostitute" themselves to be with someone who has or holds "power."

Aesthetic Attraction - Aesthetic attraction is a little like a sexual attraction except that in its pure form (not mixed with other simultaneous attractions like sex) it doesn't require sexual fulfillment. It is pure admiration of beauty.

Admiration Attraction - Admiration is like an aesthetic attraction but usually non-physical. You can admire what a person has done, or who they are, or how they handle things in life, etc. and be attracted to them for it.

Curiosity Attraction - Curiosity attraction usually leads to many partners. Especially when someone is looking to learn something or searching for some unknown factor. Many men and women will have a desire to get to know someone sexually, that they know they could not ultimately marry. Perhaps the person has a quality or two that someone would like to get to know better or learn about.

Other Vectors involved in Relationships

Time - Is the relationship ongoing, or for a limited defined length of time, or just a onetime momentary interaction?

Mutual - Is the relationship based on a mutual sexual attraction or a one way attraction, or attractions based on different vectors?

Direction of attraction - Who likes whom the most? Or is the attraction equal? When one person likes the other significantly more than the other likes them, the other usually wields the power.

How various relationships work

Platonic relationships - in our modern society, a platonic relationship is one where someone wants to be friends with someone of the opposite sex, but they do not want to have sex with that person. Platonic relationships are usually not mutual; otherwise, we just call it friends. Platonic relationships usually involve one person with a sexual attraction and one who just wants to be friends.

Prostitution - Prostitution is where you simply and overtly pay for sex. Prostitution, though prevalent, is illegal in most countries. However there are states such as Nevada in the US that have legal prostitution and countries such as Germany, Venezuela, and the Netherlands that have legalized prostitution.

There are many levels and forms of prostitution from streetwalking (which is usually considered the lowest form of prostitution involved with the most desperate people and the most unclean and unsafe) to escort services, massage parlors and Tantra lessons (these don't officially deliver prostitution but are set up so that girls who want to deliver prostitution through the service can do so), to high-class and expensive (but illegal) call-girls and brothels, and to legalized government regulated prostitution.

Prostitution is about the easiest way for a man to get sex on demand that there is. However, it is usually illegal and you may be arrested for it. Most men (at least in the US - in other countries there are some differences) report that it is a particularly unpleasant and unsatisfying form of sex - especially with its lower rank such as streetwalkers and even with legal government regulated prostitutes.

One Night Stands -- One-night stands are most commonly achieved in bars and clubs, when people are drunk and horny. These relationships don't usually last more than a night, because when you wake up (and sober up) in the morning and you see who (or what) you did it with, you want to get out of there as fast as you can and never see them again.

Friends with Privileges - these kinds of relationships come about as a result of dating someone, or knowing someone at work or school, who you come to realize just isn't right for you, but you both happen to be single without a significant other and horny every once in a while, so you get together every once in a while to satisfy sexual urges even though you know the relationship is going nowhere.

Occasionally when break ups are mutual and amicable, ex lovers will continue to have sexual relations every once in a while to satisfy sexual urges. Sometimes even divorced couples engage in sexual friendship even after they have broken up and gotten a divorce decree.

Dating with Casual Sex - These are pretty much relationships where people have sex freely with our much rules or restrictions with anyone they are dating. Most of the time people doing this have multiple partners whether simultaneously or in a row.

Lovers Only - These kind of relationships are sexual and emotional (as opposed to one-night-stands that are almost purely sexual), where both partners are looking for sexual pleasure and companionship and perhaps even friendship from the other. Sometimes these relationships involve two single people who know they are not right for any other kind of relationship (or at least one does) or married or committed people who are having extra marital affairs. In some cultures and countries, it is traditional for married partners to have lovers for sexual pleasures.

Arrangements - arrangements usually involve some sort of practical exchange between two sexual partners. A man will often financially support a woman who exclusively or non-exclusively has sex with him. But arrangements can be done for other purposes too.

Marriage to get one person citizenship papers for example would be an arrangement. The old practice of parents arranging the marriage of their children for political or economic purposes is another example. But arrangements can be done for any practical purpose that works. I once had an arrangement when I was about 28 to live with and relate to a woman monogamously so that we each could focus on our careers and get out of the "dating" scene. We agreed to stay together for about two years in order to get some things accomplished then break up and go our merry ways.

Multiple Lovers - This is when you have multiple lovers simultaneously, whether truthfully (telling them that you have other lovers) or untruthfully (lying and cheating).

Why would someone want to have multiple lovers? Well I guess this deserves a little discussion.

I personally don't think it is mentally healthy to accrue multiple lovers by lying to and cheating on your partners. However, having simultaneous multiple lovers when done truthfully has an advantage over having multiple lovers in sequence.

For one it speeds up the learning process. Rather than having five relationships in 10 years to learn about women and relationships you could probably accomplish the same thing in one year with five multiple lovers. I personally went about 5 years after I lost my virginity without learning a thing about sex with the three sequential relationships I had during that time. Then in one three-month period with the help and guidance of many multiple lovers, I became quite an accomplished lover.

Similarly, later in life, I learned more about women and relationships and myself in one four year period where I had an average of five multiple lovers at all times than I learned in the 22 year period prior to that in which I had 3 monogamous sequential relationships.

Another advantage of multiple lovers is that is protects you from making bad decisions out of scarcity. I cannot tell you how many times I actually thought I was in love and would have went for it, were it not for the fact that I had multiple relationships to keep my perspective on things; to keep me from making the fatal "horny" decision and give me time to see what was really going on.

Another advantage of multiple lovers is that it gives you a lot of confidence, makes you feel good about yourself and eventually gets you over the tendency to be focused on "sex" with women. I guarantee you when you have multiple sexual partners in abundance after a while you really start focusing on your partner's "personality" as the defining quality that you are looking for in relationships.

There may be people who do not need multiple sexual partners at all because they have no confusion in this area and know exactly what they want in a partner from the time they are born or something like that. But for people who don't have that clarity and need to learn, simultaneous multiple sexual partners is much superior to sequential multiple sexual partners in most ways. (Except maybe in the area of what your neighbor might think about you. So if you choose to do it, it may be better to keep your activities to yourself.)

Swinging - This a relationship when couples have foreplay or full sex with third or fourth parties together or swap partners with another couple or have group sex. Personally, I am monogamous when I am involved in a committed relationship so I have never engaged in swinging and I am not the person to teach you the benefits or follies of this activity. And when I am not in a committed relationship, well I'd rather have sex with just me and three girls then do the couple or group thing - but that is just me.

Open Relationships or Marriages -- These are relationships between sexual partners where the partners are allowed to have other sexual partners openly and freely.

Affairs - Affairs are commonly referred to as cheating. It is a secret relationship or relationships that you have with another while simultaneously being in a committed relationship with a partner.

Girlfriend/Boyfriend - This is the traditional non-married relationship one has with one's sexual partner as the first stage of getting to know each other before marriage. A girlfriend/boyfriend relationship would traditionally be a monogamous committed relationship, usually not living together, though girlfriend/boyfriends will sometimes end up living together before marriage and before engagement.

Living Together - This a relationship that committed couples have before or after engagement. This may come about as a test of marriage, in place of marriage (for those who don't believe in marriage) or as a practical matter to save living expenses, etc.

Marriage - The traditional long term committed monogamous relationship combining romance and finances and the rearing of children.

Now that is a summary of relationships for you to consider. You ought to know what kind of relationship(s) you are looking for when meeting, dating, and relating to women.

9) HOW TO CREATE A BETTER RELATIONSHIP

So you want a good relationship, huh? You want your girl to like sex more? You want her to understand you better? Or perhaps one of the 1000 other little items that bug guys in relationships?

Well, if you want a better relationship - here is the first rule.

Relationships are created and take continual active work to improve them. A relationship either gets better or worse, there is no static state in relationships - they either get better or worse.

If you create them, they get better. If you stop creating them, they get worse. It's that simple. And it applies to ALL relationships- work, girlfriend, kids, buddies.

Now my observation is that MOST women already know this and MOST men either DON'T know it, or if they do, they don't practice it.

So then exactly WHAT are we talking about when we talk about RELATIONSHIPS and CREATE.

Well first, let's make a distinction between casual social relationships and working productive relationships.

Webster tells us that a relationship is:

The state of being mutually or reciprocally interested
(as in social or commercial matters).

However, it is not a very good definition, because you still have a relationship with that "boss" at work who you don't like and are definitely NOT interested in and they are not interested in you, or that teacher at school who is NOT interested in you in the least or you he. So let's look at a different definition:

"A relationship exists with anyone that you co-act with towards a specific goal. "

If that "goal" is social, then of course anyone you hang with to have fun or entertainment or whatever with- you are relating to.

If that "goal" is business, then anyone you are co-acting with to get a paycheck or to make money, or whatever you do, is in a relationship with you. And of course that "teacher" you aren't the least bit interested in and who likewise is not interested in you is co-acting with you towards giving you a grade for the course - which is both your purpose and his.

So, this is a little better working definition for our purposes. If you are not working with someone towards some purpose - be it social (talking, having fun) familial (co-mingling finances, sexual fun, raising children) or business (getting paid for the work you do or products or services that you produce.) you are NOT in a relationship with that person.

The co-action doesn't even have to be direct. You can have a relationship based on a relatively unseen co-action with someone you never met. For example, the girl that works in the office in Atlanta who types up your check each week (you live in New York), well, you have a relationship with her. If she doesn't show up one day and type up your paycheck, you will realize you depend on her co-action for your own survival (pay check!)

We could even go so far as to say you have a potential relationship with people who are co-acting independently and indirectly of you, who are only related by space and time. The kid in the back of the class that you never notice, see, or talk to, by sheer proximity can stop you one day and say, "let's do homework together" or simply start asking you questions about school or class which you answer.

Your cousin in Toledo, Ohio who you never met or perhaps didn't even know existed can call you one day and say I am your cousin and you will afford him social courtesies and instant relationship that you wouldn't afford to a similar stranger.

So when you first meet a girl and are attracted to her - you are trying to establish a relationship - whether it is just for a fling (sexual fun) ongoing friendship only (companionship and sexual fun) or something more serious - like all of the above plus living together and sharing finances and raising children together.

You are hoping she will be attracted to you too, and then that will lead to hanging out fun and, in most cases, what you really want and need from a woman- sexual fun. And if this happens you have a sexual relationship.

NOW REMEMBER there is NO STATIC state in any relationship. Relationships either get better (you are relating more and having more fun or producing more desired products - happiness, contentment, personal goals, children, sex, etc.) or they get worse (you are relating less, see each other less, have less fun, have less sex, produce less products together.)

So, when we talk about CREATING a relationship we are talking about making a relationship better - more fun, more products, more togetherness, etc. And when you DON'T create a relationship the opposite happens - whether you like it or not - and there will be less fun, less togetherness, less products, etc.

NOW selecting the right person to establish a relationship with has a lot to do with it. Because you can unfortunately get with the wrong person who will not CREATE the relationship or try to make it any better. But qualifying a person for a relationship is another technology and I address that in other places, and falls more under DATING technology than RELATING technology. If you are in a relationship (even if it is with someone you probably shouldn't have gotten with in the first place.) You are going to first have to try to CREATE your way out of the bad relationship before you give up on it and move on.

WHY? Am I being moralistic here? No. I am being practical. If you got yourself into a mess, you need to learn how to do every thing right before you leave and move on, OR ELSE you will find yourself in a situation where you are NOT CREATING with the right person and then THEY WILL DUMP YOU.

So what is CREATING a relationship? CREATING a relationship is doing those things which increase attraction (both physical and mental/spiritual), communication, understanding, mutual survival, agreements between you, and the number and or quality of the products you produce together.

When you are NOT creating a relationship the attraction decrease (physical and/or mental/spiritual), the communication worsens, the understanding and mutual survival lessens, the agreements between you lessen and/or are broken, and the number and quality of products you produce together go down.

SO let's translate this into actions you can do.

Well, you probably already know how to CREATE a relationship. Most guys do it when they are romancing the girl to get her. They bring her flowers, open the door for her, assure her she looks nice (when she is worried about it), and listen to her gossip even though it bores them out of their mind. The go to the mall with her when they really hate shopping. They go to chick movies with her now and again. GET IT GUYS - you know what I am talking about - CREATING is ALL those things you do to GET THE GIRL!

(And I don't just mean traditional things like above. If you do non-traditional things to attract a woman, like I outline in EXAMPLE TWO previously, then those are the things you must do to keep attracting her.)

Now the problem is most guys do all kinds of things they DON'T like just to get the girl, so after they get her and feel comfortable in their position - THEY STOP doing all those things that they don't like.

PROBLEM IS, GUYS, THAT is the death toll for the relationship.

WHATEVER you did to GET THE GIRL you have to do MORE OF IT, more frequently, and in new and better ways to CREATE the relationship and KEEP her.

So all of this actually goes back to INTEGRITY and QUALIFYING. When DATING - Never, never, NEVER do things that you really DON'T want to do. If you don't like giving a girl flowers - DON'T - find a girl who doesn't like flowers. If you don't like opening car doors for a woman and being a gentleman, then don't be one. FIND a girl who is liberated and doesn't want a man to do that.

If your idea of romance that you can CREATE is going camping and fishing, then find a girl who thinks that is ROMANTIC too.

Believe it or not, guys, there is a girl who is just right for you. I know because I am the guy who went out on 700 dates in a year and talked to an awful lot of women. YOU don't have to compromise your integrity to get a relationship with a woman.

SO the first mistake in CREATING relationships with women is NOT FINDING the right woman for you in the first place.

The second mistake is to compromise your integrity and start doing things "to get the woman" that you aren't going to be able to continue to do AFTER you get her.

The third mistake is to STOP doing the things that got you the girl in the first place. WHATEVER got you the girl, will continue to get you the girl (with a few exceptions I won't get into now). But you are going to have to be a little creative and figure out NEW ways to do it so it doesn't become routine and boring.

SO, if you went dancing with the girl once a week when you were courting her (and she loved it) continue to go dancing with her once a week when you are married, even when you have children - hire a baby sitter. Romance your wife. But, you may need to vary it - dance with her after a romantic dinner at home. Take her to new and exciting dance places. Take dance lessons with her. Get the idea.

There are probably dozens of little things (or big things) like this you did to get her. CONTINUE to do them. Do them better. Find new ways of doing them. And find new ways to attract her. You are going to have to do this continuously, and if you want to keep her for the rest of your life, then you are going to have to do this for the rest of your life.

I'm in my fifties and I have NO PROBLEM getting a HOT YOUNG 25-year-old GIRLFRIEND. Why? Because most young guys (and a lot of older ones too) simply don't know how to CREATE a relationship as above.

WOMEN are easy to attract and seduce with CREATE. But, if you chose to attract and seduce a woman with create, you have to continue to seduce her with create as long as you want that relationship to continue.

ATTRACTION is a physical energy flow. It is not something that someone has forever - just because they were attracted to you on one or several occasions, or even long periods of time. ATTRACTION has to be continuously created. To put it simply, whatever you did to ATTRACT the girl in the first place (including seemingly negative things like being aloof and "hard to get" if that is what you did), you have to continue to do that to

CREATE a relationship. If you continuously attract the girl you are in a relationship with, the relationship will grow, get closer, and be more fun and more productive. And Oh yeah, she'll want sex just as much as you do (if not more!)

Now this is a simple description of the process. This simple explanation will help some of you, but others will need a lot more details and examples to handle complex situations.

How to Manage "Creating a Better Relationship"

In the last section, we discussed the principles of creating a better relationship. In this section, we are going to discuss the principles of managing "Creating a Better Relationship."

Now what do I mean by manage?

Well Webster gives us a workable definition:

"To exercise executive, administrative, and supervisory direction of"

To put it in a way you might understand better. To mange something is to direct it so that you achieve your purpose. So, if our purpose is to "Create a Better Relationship", how do we manage our activities so that we achieve our purpose.

Well, the best way to mange anything and to control the direction towards a purpose is by a combination of observing the statistics of the activity and planning off of that.

For example, if you are playing football and you are on the 50 yard line with a third down and 3 yards to go for a first down, you can come up with a plan to achieve your purpose much better than if you had no idea where you were at, what down it was, and how many yards to go for a first down.

Most guys are in that condition of "not knowing where they are at" when it comes to a relationship. They have no idea. If you want to win this relationship game, you have to monitor your statistics at all time - know where you are at and act accordingly. Statistics are PERCEPTION. They allow you to see where you are at in relationship with respect to your goal. Without statistics you are BLIND and stupid (like the guy who doesn't keep track of his bank account statistic (his balance) and is bouncing checks all over the place!

So, the question is what is the most important statistic for a guy to watch and monitor with respect to relationships. WRITE THIS DOWN, because you are not going to get it from any of the other Dating Guru's. The statistic you want to monitor is MOTION. Specifically MOTION TOWARD and MOTION AWAY. (See Chapter 4.)

You won't believe how important the observation of this statistic is until you start doing it. It will change your life. It is not only involved in men/women relationships it is involved in any relationship you can think of (For example, I use it extensively in sales).

Now, when it comes to women you should be watching MOTION from day one. I discovered the importance of this when I was 25 and doing the bar scene nightly, I was very shy and just stood there for about 2 months looking at people and talking to no one.

After a while, I began to watch the MOTION involved in interactions rather than the content (what people say) of interactions. That is when I became suddenly successful.

I recommend that if you haven't already read Chapter 2 (c) above you do it now:

These are excellent studies in situational techniques derived from observing motion and I will refer to them below.

And although I don't talk about the concept of motion in this section, the study of motion is how I developed these three different strategies for these three different personality types. (See Chapter 4 for a full discussion of motion.)

You see, personality even boils down to motions, these three types of girls each exhibited a uniquely different but rather common MOTION pattern in the bar scene. I simply worked out the corresponding MOTION pattern that directed and increased their MOTION vector towards me and became successful in these situations 100% of the time.

Now what most guys do in the bar scene is some arbitrary motion pattern they learned from some GURU without observing the motion at hand, or they do their own arbitrary motion pattern. The arbitrary pattern will work a percentage of times, so most guys, if they hit up on enough girls with any kind of motion, will eventually find someone it works on.

But, what makes observational technique and strategies superior is that you are not doing some arbitrary. You are doing the exact thing that works and you win 100 percent of the time across ALL Motion patterns, and ALL personality types.

There are only three basic motions a person can do with respect to you. 1) Move toward you, 2) move away from you, and 3) stay in the same place with respect to you (no motion or parallel motion).

Now when I talk about motion here with respect to a man/woman relationship I am talking about motion towards you in many ways, like:

1) Physically (a woman moves closer to you, touches you, etc.)
2) Mentally (agreement would be a motion toward, disagreement a motion away)
3) Emotionally (liking you and feeling comfortable would be a motion toward and disliking you, feeling uncomfortable with you would be a motion away)
4) Communicatively (wanting to talk to you would be a motion toward, not wanting to talk to you would be a motion away).

Then there are different channels of communication. A girl could lean into you very sexily, touch you lightly, and tell you what a bastard prick you are. If you only pay attention to the content, you could be blown away. If you only pay attention to the touch, she could blow you away. But, if you pay attention to the complex communications and all the motion vectors involved, you would know what to do.

Now these three basic motions combined with different channels of communication can get very complex as not only are there different channels of communication but there are motions within motions.

For example, my approach to these Beautiful Teases is a complex example of applying these basic motions.

When I observed these women, I noticed that they had a rather unique motion. They would approach guys and flirt with them, but if the guys flirted back or moved towards them (which MOST did) they would turn and RUN away. I then noticed that the only guys who ever got these girls were the guys who didn't respond to these girls' approaches with a motion toward, but just ignored them.

So I developed a strategy of MOVING TOWARD them (would walk over and stand next to them) but point my body AWAY from them (stand side to side not get up into their face) and I would then direct my attention AWAY from them (look at THAT girl) and emotionally my conversation would move TOWARD them as a friend and AWAY from them as a "good looking body."

It worked.

So let's get back to relationships. If you are in a relationship, the girl is either moving TOWARD you - physically, emotionally, mentally, and communicatively or she is staying in the same place with respect to you, or she is moving AWAY.

THESE ARE YOUR STATISTICS that you use to manage your relationship. You watch and observe what is she doing and the direction of her motion.

If she wants LESS sex, she is moving away. If she doesn't talk to you as much, she is moving away. If she is getting bored with you, when she use to be enthralled she is moving away.

If she wants "to talk" about things (guys hate this) she is starting to move away, but she is simultaneously moving toward you (wanting to communicate about it.)

Now what do you do about it?

Well, if you remember how I handled the Regular Gradient Girls in the barroom scene in Chapter 2(c), you will have a good start.

The gradient approach is the approach you will usually have to take to repair a relationship that is MOVING away from you. The lack of CREATE over time creates a MOTION AWAY. THE DISTANCE AWAY will determine how quickly it repairs. A year of NO CREATE could really damage some relationships and take an equal amount of time to fully repair. Others could be repaired in a few weeks. It really depends on the DISTANCE away the person has drifted AWAY during the period of NO CREATE.

It also depends on WHO has been doing the NO CREATE and is responsible for the drifting apart. If you have been creating the whole time and she hasn't, that is a lot harder to repair then if she has been creating the whole time, you haven't, and then she sort of gave up. START creating here and that one will repair real easy.

REMEMBER about gradients, as I talked about in Chapter 49 (c), and ONLY do those things which create a "motion toward' from her. It doesn't matter what you think is cool. You might think that giving her a diamond ring is real cool and should create a motion toward you, but if it doesn't, that is a STATISTIC and it tells you a lower gradient is out.

A lower gradient is just something that you have to do first before the higher gradient will work. Like in football, you usually have to get to the opponent's 40 yard line before you can consider a field goal. Trying to do a field goal when you are at your own 10 yard line is pointless.

In the bar scene example above, I had to have the "negative sex talk" with the girl before I could have "positive sex talk" - it is just the way that it is.

So don't put your feelings about things above your observations. It does not matter what you feel is good, should be good, or should work, etc. OBSERVE what makes her move toward you on the vector you are working on - physical, emotional, communication, mental - and CREATE more of that. OBSERVE what makes her move away and STOP doing that.

REAL SIMPLE - observe what makes her move toward you, CREATE more of that. Observe what makes her move away from you and STOP doing that.

Now if you just do those two simple actions on a daily basis you can make any relationship better and continue to grow and you can repair a relationship that has gone astray.

OBSERVATION, however, is not always as easy as it sounds. I have a friend who I have been telling all this stuff for years, and he still hasn't developed the ability to observe.

One night we went to a restaurant together, and I flirted with the waitress lightly. I said something like, "You have pretty eyes."

As soon as I said that, she leaned back a little, away from me, and I knew immediately she probably had a boyfriend or something. Her motion was telling me I would have to approach her on a much lower gradient if I was interested in continuing.

Well my friend didn't get it. He thought it was a great lead in for him to hit up on her and started saying all kinds of stuff to her. She began getting quite uncomfortable with us, and I finally had to kick my friend under the table to get him to stop.

When she left, I asked him "Didn't you see her lean away from me when I said that?" Well he admitted he did SEE it, but he didn't OBSERVE it or know what it meant. So, he jumped in at the wrong gradient. I got him to stop and I made the girl relax when she came back by saying, "Don't take us seriously; we flirt with ALL the girls." She laughed and then totally relaxed with us.

The point of this story being that some guys SEE motion, but DON'T observe it or interpret it correctly. If that is you, just KEEP practicing until you get it right.

The only other thing you will have to take into account in all this, is your personal integrity. Sometime when you start to really observe people and seeing what makes them move toward you, or away from you, you get into a conflict of values, interests, opinions, etc.

You may find yourself in a position that you don't want to do the things that work and make her move toward you, and she doesn't want to do the things that you would like to do to make her move toward you.

When you find yourself in that position, you are perhaps in the wrong relationship for you and you guys should sit down and really discuss your values and where each of you want to go with your lives and your relationship to see if it is worth continuing.

So now, you got two very big basics:

You have to continually create a relationship for it to continue to get better.
And you have to observe if what you are creating is making the girl move towards you are away from you. Do only those things that make her move towards you.

If you do this correctly, your girl will fall deeper and deeper in love with you as time passes. Sex will get better and better, and you will fall deeper and deeper in love with her. (Provided you got the right girl to begin with!)

"Creating a Relationship" - The Different Types of Create and Gradients

In the last section, we discussed the principles of managing "Creating a Better Relationship." In this section we are going to discuss the different types of create involved in creating relationships and one technique in particular - the use of gradients.

There are different types of create involved in relationships.

There is a type of create one must use in establishing a new relationship.

There is another type of create one must employ in moving a relationship up through its various stages - dating, boyfriend/girlfriend/living together/engaged/ married/ married with children.

There is another type of create (or pro-active lack of create) one must employ to keep a relationship at a certain stage and not have it progress.

There is another type of create one must use in order to keep the attraction between two individuals increasing and not diminishing at any level of relationship.

There is yet another form of create one must utilize when reestablishing a damaged relationship.

Then there are different kinds of relationships that people try to establish. Not everyone is looking to get married with respect any given relationship.

Different kinds of sexual relationships

- Prostitution (pay for sex)
- One night stands
- Friends with privileges
- Dating with casual sex
- Lovers only.
- Arrangements (you take care of me, I'll take care of you)
- Multiple Lovers
- Swinging
- Affairs (cheating on someone)
- Girlfriend/boyfriend
- Living together
- Engagement
- Marriage.
- Divorce (Yes some people even have sex after marriage, sort of friends with privileges phase again.)

There are also two distinct conditions we have to look at when discussing male/female relationships. The first is a condition of “opposition” or "opponents", where the love interest is an opponent. No matter where it is at, there is no agreement on the relationship and where it is going, and one person wants to take it to a different level or place than the other, who is usually just fine the way thing are.

This automatically applies to most new relationships and old relationships that are damaged or in trouble.

Now, why do I call it a condition of opposition or "opponents"? Well, because someone is usually trying to get someone, or opposed to someone. You are trying to get the girl for a girlfriend, or you are trying to get her in bed for sex, and there is some opposition. There is not complete agreement even if it is just about timing or "when." Or she is trying to get you to marry her and you don't want to yet. You are happy being her boyfriend.

The second condition is when the love interests are "team mates." They are in agreement on their relationship and where they want it to go, etc. There is no opposition here.

This applies to most good relationships where people are co-operating and in agreement on the form of their relationship be it "friends with privileges," "girlfriend/boyfriend" or "husband/wife."

Now the truth of it is, most relationships are a combination of these conditions, perhaps mostly one or the other, but it is typical that we are in opposition about some things and in complete agreement and teammates about others.

In this section I am going to discuss the first condition of "opponents" and the use of "gradients" - a major principle we use to successfully change the form of our relationship with someone and to move from one level of relationship to a higher level of relationship and to overcome opposition.

I will discuss the condition of "teammates” in the next section of this Chapter.

I talked about gradients briefly in Chapter 4(c). Let’s quickly review.

Now what do I mean by "Gradient"?

Webster says a gradient is "the rate of regular or graded ascent or descent"

Well again I feel Webster if falling a little short of a workable definition for our purposes.

For our purposes, let's just look at a "gradient" as a step on a ladder. And functionally a gradient allows us to safely go up the ladder or down the ladder one step at a time.

Now you have all been on a ladder and you know that ladders are quite workable and safe as long as you take it one step at a time. If you tried jumping up onto the fifth step of a ladder, you might have some problems getting there, and if you tried climbing or descending five steps at a time, well, you might just get hurt.

Now occasionally you could start on the second or third step of a ladder without any problem, and other times if you had some other means of ascending or descending (like your buddy lifts you up with a fork lift) you could get on or off a ladder at a higher step without any problem.

Get the picture? A gradient allows us to safely ascend or descend from one place to another.

Now when we are talking about developing or repairing or creating a relationship gradients" are the steps that allow us to safely ascend to a higher level of relationship or safely descend (yes, there are times you have to do this too) to a lower level of relationship despite any opposition to our plan.

Now the first thing you have to learn about gradients in relationships is how to see them. Gradients in relationships are usually "mental" steps and as such are not as obvious as are the steps of a physical ladder.

This may be hardest thing about using gradients for guys to learn. Learning how to see them. Most people just don't observe much. They are too use to being told by others what is right and wrong, good and bad, and simply what is and isn't.

If you want to be successful at relationships, YOU have to start observing things and become your own advisor. If you remember from the last section "How to Manage Creating a Relationship" what you have to observe are your statistics, and the main statistic to observe in a relationship is motion - "is he/she moving toward me or away from me" in response to my actions.

If you continually monitor (watch) all the actions and efforts that have a bearing on a relationship with respect to the other person you will notice that these actions/efforts either create the person moving closer (emotionally, physically, mentally, communicatively) toward you are moving further away from you in these aspects.

When I discovered the personality types in the bar scene that I write about throughout this book, I simply did so by observing motion of girls and guys in the bar, and I quickly learned how to overcome personality types that had been before hand a lot of opposition.

With the regular or "gradient girls" I discovered that I was approaching them on the wrong gradient. I would usually ask them to dance or say something nice to them (positive sex talk). Well it didn't work. It wasn't until I discovered the lower gradient of "negative sex talk" that I began having success in relating to these girls.

You see finding the right gradient turns opponents into teammates.

With the beautiful "love girl", It was the opposite. I and most guys in the bars approached them on too LOW a gradient. We weren't ready for a sexy, confident girl so we needed time to build up our courage, figure out what was going on, etc. Didn't work - by the time we built up our courage they were gone, or they were with another guy. So, I had to come into this relationship at a higher gradient. As soon as I saw them, I walked up and asked them to dance. It worked, I became a teammate rather than the lowly opposition.

The Beautiful Tease girls were a challenge. They would approach you and flirt, so you would think they were interested in you and you would approach them back on what appeared to be the right gradient - flirt, positive sex talk, show interest, after all, you knew they were interested in you. But then, when you did that, they would run away.

Well it turned out that the right gradient was to approach these girls physically (while not approaching them sexually) and to show interest and positive sex talk (but not directed towards them). If you got this gradient in and kept it in, these beautiful teases would take it from there and keep upping the sexual gradients- date, make out, petting, heavy petting until they got you in bed. But, success here depended on you keeping that ONE lower gradient in at all times. And when you did, you became a teammate and these girls did anything for you.

What do these various gradients have in common in the above examples? Nothing really, other than I observed the motion in each situation and found a lower gradient or higher gradient of approach or action that increased the motion and interest towards me, and allowed me to become a teammate rather than an opponent.

OBSERVATION is the key to success in relationships and particularly when you want to overcome opposition and establish a relationship or move it from one level of relationship to the next. OBSERVE your partner, observe how she relates to other people, her girlfriends, her guy friends, her family. What make her move closer towards them? What make her move further away from them? When does she oppose them, when does she cooperate and become a teammate?

OBSERVE sequences of action. In order to see gradients you must be able to see sequences of action.

What is a sequence of action? Well in a sequence of action one thing precedes (comes before another) - like "date/engaged/marry" or "touch/kiss/make-out/petting/sex."

OBSERVE your partner. Does she just get MAD at you? Or is there a gradient sequence there - like - you promise to do something - you screw up and forget - you won't talk about it - she gets MAD!

Or how about this one. Does she just CHEAT on you, or is there a sequence of events - like - she tells you she is unhappy but you ignore it, and don't follow up on the communication -- she keeps telling you she is unhappy and wants to see more of you but you tell her you are too busy and she needs to understand? She says she wants to talk and complains how she is unhappy and you never do anything together any more, but you don't really listen to her, you tell her she just needs to understand that you are working hard to support the family -- she tells you she needs time to herself and wants to see more of her girlfriends and you say OK because you are too busy anyway -- SHE CHEATS, and you are devastated because you didn't see it coming!

EVERYTHING happens in gradients, there are no mysteries in life when you just open up your eyes and start looking for the right things. She doesn't just up and leave you. Gradiently, you grow apart. She gives you plenty of signals of the exact gradient of "apart" you are on. You just have to learn to look.

If you start seeing sequence of events and gradients, you can do something about all this. When I saw the motion in the bar scene I refer to in my articles, I wasn't particularly bright. In fact, I had just gotten divorced and was drunk about 24 hours a day. I wasn't very bright at the time, I just happened to start looking in the right direction. No matter how smart you think you are, if you are looking in the wrong direction it won't do you any good. Even a drunk looking in the right direction can be smarter than a more intelligent man looking in the wrong direction.

Look at MOTION (away and towards). Look and see, "Do I have a teammate, here, or an opponent?" Look at sequences of action. Then when you have a problem and you don't know what to do, when you have an opposition you don't know how to overcome, when you feel uncomfortable about something, look for a different gradient (lower or higher, but usually its lower).

Here are some examples:

I use to feel uncomfortable approaching women. If I saw a hot babe, I felt like walking up to her and saying "Wow, are you hot or what?" or "Will you marry me?" or "I'm in love." Or "Hey, I just saw you over there and I'm really attracted to you."

Now before I really looked at it I thought the sequence of approach was something like this

1) First step -You have to approach the girl or she is gone forever and you lose
2) Second step -You have to tell her you are attracted to her or you won't be able to create the chance of seeing her again.

Problem is I couldn't bring myself to do it, too shy, too insecure about myself. So I would just let the opportunity pass. One day I finally sat down and applied gradients to the situation. I figured out that the real problem was I was uncomfortable with telling a hot girl exactly how much I liked her because I didn't want to face the rejection (especially in front of other people) if she responded negatively.

Now prior to this I watched guys approaching girls and observed some gradients. I observed that it didn't really matter what you said to a girl, if a girl liked you she would say something back. If a she is interested in you she will keep the conversation going, if she is NOT she will end the conversation quickly and try to get away.

So let's look at the sequence of events in this situation which added some gradient steps between 1 and 2 above.

1) First step -You have to approach the girl or she is gone forever and you lose
2) Second step - You have to say something to her or someway attempt to engage her in a conversation or she probably won't do it herself.
3) Third step - Say something neutral that will not embarrass you are be obvious to people around that you are hitting on her.
4) Watch her response - does she try to keep the conversation going?
5) If she doesn't, let her go - no harm no foul - nothing to be embarrassed about after all you just asked her for the time. But if she keeps the conversation going and appears to be interested in doing so go to next step.
6) Keep the conversation going yourself. At some point add a slight "flirt" and see how she responds - something like "Wow, you have really pretty eyes."
7) If the slight flirt doesn't push her away, take it to the next level. Tell her she is an interesting person and you would like to talk to her some more but you have to go. Get her phone number and/or email.
8) You have achieved step 2 (letting her know you are attracted to her)in the first example above because women are use to subtle communications, and she now knows you are interested in her and thinks you are really cool because you did it in normal way (not the usual guy way - "Wow, you are so beautiful!")

With this one observation, I worked out a gradient strategy that forever handled my uncomfortable feelings and shyness. My shyness was really about me not wanting to look stupid by getting shot down by some girl in front of other people. When I observed the motion between men and women and that it really didn't matter what you said to a girl (if she is interested she will manage to keep the conversation going). I realized I didn't need to tell a girl that I liked her and was attracted to her on the approach.

So my best pick up line became and still is today, guys, "Hi!"

Works like a charm. And this LOWER gradient of approach eliminates what I was really afraid of - looking stupid by putting my heart on my sleeve and having some girl stomp all over it.

Situationally, every relationship, every problem, and every person is different so there is no cookie cutter model here of how to apply "gradients." But, it starts with OBSERVATION and that means internal observation as well as external.

Whenever I feel

1) Like I don't want to confront something; or
2) Uncomfortable and want to leave; or
3) Blocked and frustrated because I can't get over the opposition
4) Or just can't figure out something,

I have trained myself to immediately stop and start looking for a lower gradient way to tackle the problem, opposition, or whatever. Since I have done this, I've always figured out a lower gradient that works 100% of the time.

If at any time one of the gradients fail, look for more gradients between the last successful gradient and the one that failed.

Be creative in what you consider a gradient. There are mental, communicative, physical, and emotional steps and sometime they intertwine.

For example, here are some gradients that I have employed in various situations:

I've pretended to be drunk and said something really nice about someone when they could overhear me. Why? Because just telling them something nice was the wrong gradient. They wouldn't have believed me. They considered that people only spoke what was really on their mind when they were drunk. So, this was the lower gradient that solved my problem.

I pretended to be mad in order or have a meaningful conversation. I had a girlfriend who didn't believe I cared when I communicated in my calm rational way. She believed that people only cared when they were emotional. Yelling and screaming meant I cared. Calmness didn't. So I faked anger and yelled and screamed at her and she loved it. I remember her exact words (even though it was about 30 years ago) - "Now that's communicating!"

I once mutually broke up with a girl I had been dating for 3 years, and then after a couple of weeks decided it was a mistake and that I wanted her back to give it a better try. Meanwhile, unbeknownst to me, she had met and hooked up with a childhood sweetheart and was talking marriage.

Well, to make a long story short, I got her back. (It took me three months of applying gradients and everything else I know - so don't let the Dating Guru's tell you to write off the ex if you don't want to.)

But, there was an interesting key gradient I applied in the very beginning when I decided I wanted her back and she told me all about the new guy, etc.

We had a four-hour conversation on the phone. It was going bad as she told me all this stuff about the new guy, and how he was her childhood sweetheart and they were talking marriage, etc. but I decided I wasn't going to let her off of the telephone until I got a positive "gradient" of agreement out of the conversation that I could build on. After four hours of going lower and lower on gradients, I finally got her to admit and agree there was a 1% chance I could win her back.

I remember those words well, too. I said "Tell me there is not a 1% chance I can win you back and I will hang up the phone right now." "I can't say that," she said. "There's probably a 1% chance."

That was all that I needed. I knew where I stood and what I had to overcome. Building on that gradient of agreement, I slowly built myself back into her life (and him out of it.)

There was a time that I felt uncomfortable and unsure about suggesting intimacy or making a move with certain types of girls. I came up with a multiple-choice question to get around my own uncomfortableness as a lower gradient. Rather than say, "hey, we have been out on three dates now, do you want to mess around or something." I simply said what would you like to do tonight? A) Go to a movie? B) Go out to dinner? or C) watch TV at my place and cuddle?

They always answered C and I took it from there.

The above examples are examples of using gradients to handle your own considerations but there are also plenty of ways you can use gradients to handle other people's opposition. I've gone out with tons of beautiful women, and 99% of them told me there would never have a relationship with some guy that approached them on the street no matter how attracted they were to him

Knowing this I never hit up on women on the street in a flirting manner. (Unless they work in a store or restaurant that I can come back to - then I will out and out flirt.)
I developed a gradient approach that works well

1) Approach them about something (see my "Hi" technique above)
2) Find or create some future involvement (a reason to contact her again) on a non-sexual mutual interest ("Hey, I have a great article I can email you on that" or "I know a place that has jeans that you will love. I forget the name but I have it at home. I'll call or email it to you when I get home"
3) Establish myself non-sexually and either let them hit up on me, or then make my move when they no longer perceive me as some guy they met on the street.

Establishing future is a key "lower gradient" that you should shoot for when first meeting women. Telling her how beautiful she is (especially if she is) and how much you like her will get you nowhere. Finding a nonsexual reason why she should talk to you again will get her to actually return that phone call.

When you are interested in younger women, don't hit up on them sexually. That will blow them away. Too high a gradient. Use the lower gradient of non-sexual friendship.

Younger women appreciate an older man's maturity. Give them a chance and a reason to get to know you without scaring them away with sex, and if they like you and start hanging with you, sooner or later they'll get horny and make the first move. Always let younger women make the first move when there is a significant age difference.

In relationships, I've had to use gradients when there is an argument or disagreement. You cannot handle anything or repair a relationship if you cannot communicate about the problem. The lower gradient, though, is that you cannot communicate to someone if you do not feel comfortable and safe telling them things relevant to the discussion. Or if you don't feel safe talking to them in general.

So often I have found that before you can handle something by talking about it, you actually have to handle "talking and communicating" as a subject. Discuss why you don't feel safe communicating your deepest thoughts and feelings to your partner and perhaps make up some rules to handle that.

If you don't feel safe talking about your problems with your partner, then talking about "talking" has to be the lower gradient conversation. Clear that up, make it ok to talk to your partner, and then tackle the problem

And when talking about talking doesn't work, then you have to lower the gradient again and just shut up and spend some time being with that person and try to build up your affection for each other again.

Don't get into anything heavy, just do things you both enjoy, spend quality time together and try to restore the feelings and attraction you once had for each other. After a while, you will start to feel better about yourselves and will be ready to tackle that talk about talking.

And after that talk about talking, keep the quality time going and eventually you will be able to tackle the problem itself.

Your Love Interest as Your Teammate

In the last section, we were discussing some more of the principles of creating a relationship. Specifically we got into some detail on creating a relationship when you are in the condition of "opponent." When someone is not actively trying to create the same kind of relationship you are.

In this section, we are going to focus on the other condition. Creating a relationship when you have someone who is an active "teammate," working for the same goal you are.

When you have a partner who is an active teammate, working for the same goal in the relationship that you are, you are in the best condition you could be in. If you don't mess it up or screw it up, your relationship should grow in the direction you want it to grow and be a healthy relationship for years and years, even a lifetime if that is desired. Screwing up a healthy relationship, if you are lucky enough to have one, is actually hard to do, but believe me there are some guys who do it.

What are the major mistakes the guys make to screw up a healthy relationship?

Well here are five of the most common basic mistakes.

1) Cheating.
2) Not continuing to treat her as the opponent and win her over. (Otherwise known as Romance.)
3) Not continually creating a common opponent to fight as teammates.
4) Not continuing to monitor the goals and purposes of the team and make sure that they are still in unison.
5) Not making sure she continues to do all of the above too.

Now to create a relationship with a willing partner who wants the same thing as you do, all you have to do is continue to create romance, continue to be teammates against a common opponent (and not turn on each other for lack of a "real opponent"), continue to stay in communication with each other as you grow and change (to create staying "on the same page"), continue to be teammates and not become the enemy (by cheating or some such thing) and finally make sure your partner continues to do all of these things too.

1) Cheating - In most cases, as soon as you cheat, you become the enemy. You are no longer working as teammates for the same thing. You have a hidden agenda and you are not working for the best interest of the team.

(I say in most cases, because there are societies and couples who agree that cheating -or extra-marital sex - is ok in certain situations, and under prescribed conditions. In that event you would not be the enemy if you kept to the agreed upon “cheating” behavior. But, for most of us in this US culture, cheating is a broken agreement and you DO become the enemy to the team.)

Now my opinion on cheating is simple and it is based on practicality not morality issues. You shouldn't get married or in a serious relationship until you have the ability to commit to a monogamous relationship.

There are plenty of girls who are not ready to commit to a serious relationship. So if you are not ready it would be better to find someone else who is not ready and work out a relationship that involves non-monogamous sex together.

When I was about 25 and still in my first marriage, I had an older friend who was about 35. He was pretty messed up when it came to relationships, and didn't have his act together, but he had no problem getting sex.

He once told me something that I remembered and applied later on when I got divorced. He said that he had finally learned that the "Best Lie is the TRUTH." He said that he use to lie to women and make all kinds of promises and say things he didn't mean just to get sex. Then one day he discovered if he just told them the truth - that he was messed up, unreliable, and would probably cheat on them - he started getting more girls that were willing to have sex with him.

I am a monogamous man when I am married or in a committed relationship. In between relationships when I am not quite ready to get back into another one yet, I am not monogamous. I do what I want, but I never lie about it. I tell the girls I am dating up front that I am not ready for a committed relationship and that I have sex with other people. And I have never found it hard to get women to still have sex with me when I say this.

The point of all this is, if you are not ready for marriage or a committed relationship, don't get involved with someone who is, and don't pretend like you are - not even to (and especially not even to) yourself. You'll turn your teammate into an enemy overnight. Get my eReport on "How I Got 700 Dates in One Year" (http://datingtorelating.com/inc/sdetail/230) and work out whatever it is remaining in your system that keeps you from being monogamous.

Believe it or not, if you were to have sex with a different woman every night for 6 months like I have a couple of times in my life (in between serious relationships), I guarantee you two things: 1) you'll become a fantastic lover and really know how to please your girl when you do settle down; and 2) you'll value personality more and won't find it difficult to settle down with the right girl after a stint like that.

Without being moralistic, breaking an agreement to be monogamous with your girl and cheating on her doesn't get you anywhere. If sex with multiple women is what you want, you can have more sex with more women without cheating on anyone by telling the truth. Cheating in a committed relationship is a false sense of accomplishment. It means you are unhappy and insecure and a whole bunch of other negative things. So, if you feel like cheating, there is something wrong.

And as soon as you get that feeling, you need to sit down with your mate, talk things out. And if you can't resolve things so that you are back on the same team again then you are in the wrong relationship for you and you probably need to get out of that situation and date extensively until you work whatever sexual issues you have out of your system - so you can actually have a serious, monogamous relationship.

2) Now another way guys wreck a good teammate relationship and contribute to the girl cheating on them is to stop romancing the girl.

Now remember this girl was at one time an opponent, someone you had to win over to your way of thinking, before she agreed to become your girlfriend or wife, etc. - That's what all the flowers and candies, and door "holding" and chick flicks and "listening" was about - you were trying to win the game and "score" the girl.

So, you did. And now you think that game (you didn't really like it did you) is over and you don't have to do that anymore. Now that she is the girlfriend or wife, you don't have to play that "flowers' and "door opening" game anymore. Well guess what guys! You are wrong.

All those things you did to impress her and get her, worked. These things created "attraction" towards you. Now that you have secured this agreement for her to be your girlfriend or wife and enter into this new game of “teammates" it doesn't mean that the old game is over.

You see building or creating a relationship is sort of like building a house. You lay the foundation for a house then you build the first floor. When the first floor is complete, you don't go and tear down the foundation. If you do, the first, second, third, etc. floors will all come tumbling down with it.

Same thing with a relationship. Whatever you did to get the girl, whatever you did to attract her in the beginning is your foundation. You can't go tearing it down the minute you get the first floor built and move in.

It simply won't work.

If anything, as you continue to build onto your house, you have to strengthen your foundation to support the additional structure.

Same thing with a relationship. As you move from dating to girlfriend to engaged to marriage to children you are simply adding on to the structure and you are going to have to keep that original foundation and make it even stronger.

That means figuring out new things to do together, new ways to have fun, new sexual play so that it doesn't get boring. (Check out the Free Mini-Course on my site - "How to be a Great Lover.")

3) Now once you move from the "opponent" stage of a relationship where you are trying to WIN the girl over, you enter a stage where you are teammates mostly (but remember still keep those opponent things going to win the girl into continually being attracted to you)

In the “teammate” stage you are in agreement. You are a couple and you are approaching the world together as a team. Now, depending on your type of relationship agreement, that can be anything from just creating mutual pleasure together (like sex, or hanging out) to combining your finances and taking on the world financially together to improve your mutual lot, to deciding to take on "having kids" and raising them to the standards that you both agree on.

Now the thing is as you start working together as a team and start "winning" you can't forget that the process or working together as a team is more important than the things you obtain as a team. Teamwork is like "glue" that holds you together.

Sometimes when a couple achieves some of the goals that are the objects of their teamwork, they forget to replace those goals with new ones. Sooner or later if you don't replace old goals with new ones you run out of things to work together on.

So often a couple gets engaged, gets married, has children, gets a nice house, gets a nice car and then stop setting goals and their teamwork disappears.

Sometimes it doesn't even go that far. Sometimes they both have a simple goal like moving in together. They do that and then stop creating team projects. Like the things that you did to attract her, working together to achieve goals and solve problems is the expanded foundation of a relationship. As long as you keep doing it and set new goals to accomplish you will continue to create a healthy satisfying relationship.

Goals don't always have to be mutual goals. Sometimes a couple helps each other on personal goals. They work together as a team to get her to lose 10 pounds. They work together as a team to get him a better job.

Doing that CREATES the relationship in a healthy manner. Telling your girl you'd better lose 10 pounds or I am out of here doesn't. Telling the guy he'd better get a better job or you are gone doesn't create a relationship either. These kinds of attitudes make you "enemies" or "opponents" again.

Mutual goals are common "opponents" and make you teammates fighting against your obstacles to achieving your goals.

I can go on and on and on, on this topic, but I think you get the point. CONTINUALLY setting goals and working on those goals as a team helps to CREATE a relationship. STOP doing this and the relationship will star falling apart.

4) Now to continually monitor these goals you set as a team, this means communication. You have to talk to your partner and continually monitor where they are with respect to your mutual and their and your personal goals. People change and grow. You can't assume the girl your married 3 years ago is the same girl today. You can't assume the things that she considered important and wanted to work on with you 3 years ago, 1 year ago, even 6 months ago are still the goals she has today.

Communicate! Talk! Listen! You have to continually find out where you are. If you keep communication in then you won't' have any surprise. If you assume she is the same (when she isn't) then you will be surprised one day when you exclaim "I don't know who you are anymore" as she walks out the door or cheats on you.

5) Finally, you have to get your girl to do all of these things too. One person creating a relationship is better than none, but two people creating a relationship is a cinch for success.

Best time to talk about all this is early on in your relationship so you are both on the same page with create from the early days. But, anytime is better than no time. It is never too late. Even if you aren't "newlyweds", talk now!

If you do all the above things, you and your partner just may have a chance to create a continually growing, healthy relationship.

10) SEDUCTION

The Art of Seduction - A Classic Example

When we talk about seduction, we are talking about an art that is quite often misunderstood and quite easily confused with manipulation, trickery or deceit. Seduction can have a negative connotation, in fact the dictionary says:

> "Seduction is the process of deliberately enticing a person into an act. It can be used seriously or jokingly, frequently refers to sexual behavior and may refer to an act that the other may later regret and/or would normally not want to do."

In this Chapter, however, I am using seduction as a way of creating attraction perhaps where there is none. If done properly there is no regret - just attraction and romance.

Seduction as I define and use it, entices a person to make the first desired move. Using seduction to get someone into close proximity so you can force yourself upon them, is not a correct use of seduction. Perhaps we should give it another name such as deceit or trickery or manipulation.

RELATIONSHIPS require the correct definition of seduction. You can trick someone into having sex with you once, but not on an ongoing basis.

Seduction requires gradient steps of agreement. Assuming that the first step is not something that a person would readily agree to, you must break down the complete seduction into steps that a person can or will gradiently agree to one by one. Only moving onward to the next step when they are completely comfortable with the prior step.

The whole art of seduction is contained in the ability to perceive and apply these gradient steps, and to adjust steps on the fly when they are not working by creating yet smaller gradients to replace any particular step that is not working.

The first time a woman seduced me is a good example of gradient seduction. It went like this.

I went out on a first date with a girl I wasn't very attracted to. I was in the middle of a divorce, still not moved out of our apartment, sleeping on the living room couch. I really didn't want to go home at night, and would stay out as late as I could or stay somewhere else if someone let me.

So I went out with this girl who I had met several years earlier that I knew liked me and who use to be really hot. Only problem was she gained some weight so she wasn't as hot looking anymore and after going out with her and dancing for a couple of hours, I really wasn't all that jazzed about her personality either. Bottom line - sex with her wasn't on my mind and I would have turned her down if she had come out and asked me or suggested it.

She really wanted to "jump" me, however, and this is how she went about seducing me.

Step 1) She invited me up for some tea when I was dropping her home. I didn't really want to go home so any excuse to stay out later was ok with me. I said "Sure."

Step 2) She began to ask me about my marriage and divorce and with a little female intuitiveness quickly saw my weakness - that I didn't want to go home. She point-blank stated - "You don't want to go home, do you." I said "No."

Step 3) She offered me her back bedroom and said I could sleep there tonight no strings attached. Of course, I agreed. This was exactly what I was looking for. We talked some more and then she went a got some extra blankets to make my bed.

Step 4) As we walked into the extra bedroom she remarked how cold it was in there and said she was sorry but she did not have an extra heater. Then she came up with a better idea. She had an extra separate bed in her "warm" bedroom. I could sleep there.

Well it was really cold in the spare bedroom and that sounded good to me. I just wanted a nice warm place to go to sleep. So I said "OK."

Step 5) She prepared the spare bed in her room as we talked some more. It was on the other wall away from her bed and I was totally comfortable with it. She then asked me if I wanted some more hot tea before we went to bed. I said ok and we went back out to the kitchen. We talked some more as we were waiting for the tea.

"Do you ever get lonely?" she asked. "Of course" I said. "Sometimes" she said, "I just want to cuddle up to someone. I miss not having a boyfriend to cuddle up to at night." "Yeah," I said. Then, after a little more prepping me with loneliness conversation, she asked, "Do you want to just cuddle up together tonight? I won't attack you." She added. Well it sounded good. Just cuddle... "Sure." I said.

Step 6) We are laying down in her bed together, just cuddling and talking a little for maybe 15 minutes or so. Suddenly, she announced she couldn't take it anymore, ripped off her night gown and "jumped" me. [Now if a guy did this to a girl this probably wouldn't have been cool, but given she was the girl and I was the guy. It worked. She had me in her bed. She was fully naked. She was yanking on my body parts...well what's a guy to do?]

Now that WAS seduction. Pure and simple. I had no intention to have sex with her, but she wanted me and she got me. Her only mistake was the last part. She used force. It worked that night, but I never had sex with her again. What she should have done was gotten me to jump her. Then she would have had a better chance for a relationship.

She could have probably accomplished that with a few more steps like this: Announce she was too hot, take off her clothes, and cuddle with me naked for a while. Then maybe start kissing me gently as we cuddled. That probably would have done it for me.

This is a good example of actual seduction technique, but it is also an example of what not to do if you want to seduce someone into a relationship. Don't use force! You can't seduce a person into a relationship with force. The last step of her example was not seduction but trickery and deceit. However, the framework of what she did overall was classic.

Seduction - Short and Long Term Techniques

In the last section I gave you a classic example of how a woman whom I had no interest in, seduced me into a one-night stand. It was a great example except for one thing. On her last step, she used force rather than seduction. This resulted in a one-night-stand but no relationship.

Let's retread the definition of "the art of seduction" for a moment:

Seduction, as I define it, requires gradient steps of agreement. Assuming that the first step is not something that a person would readily agree to, you must break down the complete seduction into steps that a person can or will gradiently agree to one by one. Only moving onward to the next step when they are completely comfortable with the prior step.

Seduction as I use it, entices a person to make the first desired move. Using seduction to get someone into close proximity so you can then force yourself upon him or her is not a correct use of seduction. Perhaps we should give it another name such as deceit or trickery or manipulation.

But although I never saw the girl who seduced me again. I learned from what she did that night, and I began putting little seduction gradients into my dating routine. One of the best relationship seductions I came up with was a variation of what had been done to me. I would go out on a first date. Take the girl home. Ask if she had some tea or something to drink as an excuse to get invited in.

I would talk for a while and then announce I was too tired to drive home and ask if I could crash the night at her place. Now since there was some level of mutual attraction going on this would invariably lead to her saying "You can sleep in my bed with me, but you can't have sex."

I would agree to those terms, and then I would keep my word and go to sleep. In the morning the girl would always tell me how she expected me to jump her anyway and how different I was from all the other guys she met, and I would simply respond "Well, you told me not to."

The girls were so impressed with my control that the next night they would jump me as soon as I got into bed with them. This worked 100% of the time.

Now this was a simple seduction but it was a real pure seduction without the use of force. These girls liked me and had sex with me again and again.

When seduction is done right without any force, people don't know you are seducing them and they don't know they were seduced. They just like what happened.

When you use force people feel deceived, tricked and have regrets about their actions. You may get what you want for the moment but you won't get a good relationship with improper seduction.

Seduction can be a complex, multi-step process (usually when resistance is high) like the first example of the girl who seduced me. Or seduction can be a simple 1 or two step process when resistance is low (like the girls who let me "only sleep" with them.)

Seductions can take minutes, hours, days, weeks or years, depending on the complexity.

Here are some more examples of simple 1 or 2 step one night seductions.

When I was young (25 or so) I use to laugh at how powerful one technique was. I simply found out where the best restaurant in town was. I would call up a girl for a first date whose number I had gotten from meeting her in a bar or on the street and I would chat and ask them if they would like to go out. When I got the girls who would say they were busy….you know the "I have to wash my hair" routine, etc. ..I would say "Too bad, because I was going to take you to ..."(I would name the fancy restaurant) and within a few seconds they would be hemming and hawing and finding a way to back out of what they previously said.

Not only did this routine get me the date with the "elusive" girl, but they would always have sex with me as sort of a "Thank you for dinner at the nicest restaurant I have ever been to" gesture.

Another example of a mini seduction routine is nudity. I have had many girls seduce me with nudity. It usually goes like this. You go to pick them up for a date. They just got home and still have to take a shower. They jump in the shower but continue to talk to you and leave the bathroom door open. Then they say they can't hear you come closer, so you step into the bathroom to chat. They eventually turn off the shower and step out either nude or with a towel that drops off shortly after.

…Then there is the girl who lets you sleep over. She tells you, you can't have sex with her, takes off all her clothes and gets into bed totally naked.

I've used these same nudity techniques with women and they work just as well. If they are the right gradient….and perhaps IF you have a hot body. Do not get sexual, though. Just casually let them see you nude.

All seductions use gradients.

The whole art of seduction is contained in the ability to perceive and apply these gradient steps, and to adjust steps on the fly when they are not working by creating yet smaller gradients to replace any particular step that is not working.

Read the examples of the "Love Girls," "Gradient Girls," and "Beautiful Teases." These are seduction techniques at work. They use gradients. Even the "Love Girl" technique is a gradient technique. It just seduces at a higher gradient.

But not all seductions are accomplished in a night. There are quite a few "Hot Women" that require ten to fifteen dates before they will go to bed with you. Most guys don't make it past the first date with them, or past three or four dates with them, because the guys are not seducing. Rather they are demanding, or wussies, or just being a little too eager or expecting.

Some seductions can be very complicated. When you are going after the girl of your dreams and she is totally not interested in you because you are too fat, too old, or too ugly, it can be a challenge. To seduce a girl who likes you but wants to be "friends only" can be a challenge.

I once won an ex-girlfriend back with seduction technique. We had a mutual break up and then she started dating another guy. Meanwhile I changed my mind and decided I wanted her back. But to complicate things the new guy was one of her childhood friends that she knew very well, and before I could even get started on my seduction, they were engaged.

Man did I have my work cut out for me.

Much too complicated to go into full detail here, it took me three months but I did it. I worked hard for those three months constantly planning, plotting seductions, and gradient things to do every day. Slowly over the three months I went from being just-friends to non-sexual affinity (sleeping over at her house in the same bed occasionally), to close mental/emotional confidant as her relationship with the other guy started falling apart, to non-sexual roommates, to lover/boyfriend again. Here are some of the long-term seduction principles that emerged from that relatively long-term seduction.

Long-term seductions usually have a long-term resistance built in. The girl has a boyfriend, or she considers you too fat, ugly, or old to date, or all of the above. If you are creating a long-term seduction with someone who absolutely has no interest in you, it has to go like this:

1) Establish a friendship first. Now you have to be cool. You can't do things that will scare people away. If you know she is not interested in you that way, don't let on that you are interested in her that way. It won't help anything at this stage. One of the coolest techniques I've used over the years at college and other places to make an instant rather tight friendship bond is to help someone when they are really in need.

You know someone is sick. You pay them a visit. Bring them some chicken soup. Offer to do a few chores for them, etc. Don't be needy. Don't hang around. Quick visit. Help them and leave. Tell them if they need any more help just to call. People love stuff like that and know that you are really a caring person and would make a good friend.

2) Become real close friends. Talk about intimate details of your life. Get them to do the same. Get beyond the superficial stage of friendship. Let this person really get to know you and who you are, and you get to know them. Keep your attraction to her physically off the line. Don't mention it. Talk about her personality and why you like her as a person. Remember to watch motion. If she is moving toward you, you are doing the right things. Keep it up and do more. If she is moving away from you, you are doing the wrong things so stop right away.

For example, if she continually wants to hang out with you and do more and more things. That is motion toward. If she starts giving you less and less time, that is motion away. If you can get past this stage successfully, you have a good chance at a relationship if you can get physical. This is a crucial stage. You should be best friends by the end of this stage, or at least her best male buddy, but with a closeness factor no less than any of her female friends.

3) Get physical. This has to approached very carefully and very gradiently depending on how far away you are on the attraction vector. If you are absolutely repulsive to the other person it is one thing. If you are just "neutral" are just "ok" or not "real hot" to the other person it is a different story.

In either case you still have to get close. But do it for awhile then move away. Make sure you are the one to move away before she does. Do things like stand close to show her something. Lean in to see something. Do things that require closeness like amusement park rides etc. Never be sexual in any of your movements unless she originates the sexuality. Especially true if you are on the "repulsive" end of things to begin with.

In other words if you are just friends then do closeness things but don't try to hold her hand or kiss her sexually, etc., until she originates such things. But if she starts holding your hand romantically everywhere you go, then it would be time to up the gradient to a light romantic kiss.

This is a complicated step. I could write an article about it by itself. In a long-term seduction, it goes slow. Long-term seductions always have a high degree of resistance because the other person is resisting your looks, age, or personality or because they are in a relationship with another person already. In any case, the person does not want to get sexual with you at all.

So your actions have to be geared first towards making them comfortable just being close to you. Often that entails handling their consideration that if they get close to you, you WILL try to get sexual. So you must get close to them and specifically NOT get sexual to show them it is safe and OK to get close to you physically.

Once that is done, then getting close takes on the purpose of romance without being overtly sexual or romantic. You want the girl to start thinking about you and fantasizing about you physically without scaring her by getting too close physically so that she begins to back off. You want to maintain that right degree of "socially accepted" closeness to fit whatever situation she and you are in until she one day changes the consideration that prevents her from being sexual with you. (Drops the boyfriend, loses the consideration that you are too ugly, etc.)

When this happens coupled with the fact that she has been thinking about or fantasizing about being closer to you or sexual with you, she will immediately originate the next step. The most important things here are patience and observation. You must have patience and never overstep the closeness or get more sexual than she can allow. You must also be very observant to know what is going on with her and in her mind. If she enjoys being close to you even though she can't express it, you must observe that and know that she is thinking about it and you later on.

Often being physical means developing semi-sexual activity whenever you can, while denying it. Graduate your physicalness to hugs, polite social kisses, hold her hand to "read her palm," etc. If she ever suspects that you like her - deny it. Only do things that are socially accepted amongst "friends" and they can be easily denied and turned around. Say "No, I don't think of you that way. I'm just affectionate that way with all my friends. But WHY are you thinking that? What is on your mind?"

Often such a question will open up her feelings that she has been trying to hide. Don't be too eager even if she says she likes you. Be patient. Keep doing the things that worked. They got you this far. Don't blow it now with a sudden change of character. Always let her take the lead on what to do next. Always match her level of interest. Don't exceed it by much. Let her originate the next step.

If she says, “Sometimes I wonder if we could be a couple." Admit they you have had the same thought, but DON'T come back and say "WOW, like I'm totally in love with you!" It might scare her. Keep the conversations going in that direction. If you have done your best friend gradient right you can say something like "Sometimes I wonder if there is any way we are NOT compatible. Did you ever notice we get along on everything?" Use gradients continually.

If you do the above steps right, you will eventually seduce the girl. However, depending on her considerations, long-term seductions can take awhile.

My second wife seduced me over a long term. I was not attracted to her at all when I met her. But I really liked her as a friend. She worked the friend thing for over two years, then let it slip that she liked me when she got drunk one night at a party. She even got a little physical with me when she was drunk.

We were so close and such good friends, that it didn't scare me away. But even though I wasn't attracted to her physically, I knew I could have her. I also liked her very much. After two years of knowing her, I began to have little sexual fantasies about her when I broke up with my girlfriend. Then I originated to her "Let's have a one-nighter."

That is all I intended. I was a typical male. I knew I could get her and just wanted to satisfy my curiosity once. But the one night was so good, that it led to an extended one-nighter relationship.

Within three months we moved in together for practical reasons, but I still had 100% certainty that I would never marry her. She was just too plain looking for me. I was only use to and interested in marrying a "Hot" girl.

Within another year, I started wanting to handle my own considerations about her looks, because I realized I really liked her personality and was totally comfortable with her. I wanted to fall in love with her. I eventually totally handled my own considerations and proposed to her and I was totally in love when I did it.

She got what she wanted, and it took her three years to get it. I went from not even thinking about her sexually, to thinking about her sexually, to having sex with her but not intending to get serious, to living with her but not intending to marry her, to wanting to handle my considerations about marrying her, to actually marrying her.

Seduction….very powerful….use the steps above.

Seduction Qualities on a First Meeting or Date

We have talked about various aspects of seduction, but in this section let's talk about seduction qualities. What you can do physically and non-verbally to seduce a woman while you are trying to meet her or on that first date with her.

Previously I have defined seduction as:

> A way of creating attraction perhaps where there is none. If done properly there is no regret just attraction and romance.

This still applies to what I will be talking about here. But I have also said that seduction requires gradient steps of agreement. Assuming that the first step is not something that a person would readily agree to, you must break down the complete seduction into steps that a person can or will gradiently agree to one by one. Only moving onward to the next step when he or she is completely comfortable with the prior step.

However, this time I am talking about a different kind of seduction. A seduction that gets people thinking sexy and wanting to have sex with you and does not necessarily need to be applied in gradients.

The goal of this type of seduction is just to get a woman attracted to you and to think about you in a sexy way.

This form of seduction can be used in tandem with the other form of seduction, which has another goal in mind. Like performing the sex act or creating a relationship.

There are certain qualities that a man can exhibit that seduce women. If you exhibit these qualities from the first moment that you meet a woman, you have a better chance of seducing her into a relationship with you.

1) Posture- posture is one of the first things that a woman can see -even from a distance. Stand straight. Stand tall. Women will notice you from a distance. If you don't have good posture, start working on it. Watch actors on TV and in movies. Look at the men that women consider sexy. Look at their posture.

2) Motion - how you move, the way you move is another attribute that women can see from far away. Slower deliberate motions are usually more seductive than fast non thought out motion. Again watch movies, look at the men that women consider sexy. How do they move? What are there motions? Observe and learn. Imitate.

3) Dress well - How a man dresses can totally be seductive to a woman. It is a statement about you and your personality. Like posture and motion, dress can be seen from far away. Different types of women like different styles. Go to the mall, go to a party, go to church, go to work, and look at women you are attracted to and watch how the guys they are with are dressed.

Now the above are things that you can do to seduce women from a distance, to stand out and to be noticed from afar. As you approach a woman, as you get closer, the following attributers come into play.

4) Use your eyes, your smile - As you approach a woman, as you get a little closer, your eyes and your smile will come into play. Flirt with your eyes. Look at her and let her know you are interested. Don't be shy and look away. Let her be the shy one. A genuine smile can be very seductive. If you like a woman, smile at her. Use it throughout your conversation but don't overdo it. Don't fake smile. It is better to do nothing than fake smile.

5) Be Clean and well groomed - even if you have a rocker look or a biker look or whatever be clean. No one (except other dirty people) want to have sex with someone who is filthy or dirty.

6) Smell good - You don't have to use old spice or anything, but shower before you go out. Some people have body odor even after they shower. Know if you are one and then use deodorant and cologne as necessary. Gargle, use breath mints. Again, some people's breath smells even after they gargle etc. Know if you are one. Smoker's breath smells and tastes horrible to a non-smoker. Some smokers even smell from as much as 20 feet away. Usually they are unaware of it. Be aware of your smell. Ask friends. Take care of all these things before you go out on a date or on the prowl. A good smell will attract and even seduce a woman.

As you move even closer to a woman, as in a conversation or in a date, there are more things you can do to be seductive to a woman.

7) Move in close to a woman. Invade her personal space just a little and briefly, then back off. Use an excuse. Don't just do it arbitrarily. Show her something, then move away. Notice if she likes it - notice whether she lets you move close or she moves away as you move closer. If she lets you move close, she is liking it. Brush up against her accidentally. Bump her lightly if you are walking together. If you are on a date, hold her hand as you walk together.

8) If you are on a date, sitting down talking to each other, use your hands expressively. Touch her lightly now and again, as you talk. When you feel more comfortable with her, if she is responding to everything else you are doing, take her hand play with her fingers. Always touch then withdraw.

9) When you are done with the date and it is time to say goodbye or goodnight, do it with a kiss. That puts the romance right there. But use all of your attributes. Move in slow and deliberately, confidently smile at her and kiss her lightly on the lips. If she responds, kiss her again but this time run your fingers lightly through her hair on the side of her head down the back of her neck as you kiss her, then withdraw your hand down her neck and down her shoulder.

Then say goodnight, knowing she will dream of you tonight.

11) ALTERNATIVE RELATIONSHIPS -- LOVERS, MULTIPLE LOVERS AND ARRANGEMENTS

In this section, we are going talk about how to establish or create certain types of relationships that I get questions about all the time. - Lovers, Multiple Lovers, and Arrangements.

One of the problems that guys have in general with sex and relationships with women is "integrity" - specifically maintaining their integrity. Basically guys will lie to get laid. They will say anything they have to, to get laid, and then they will sing a different tune later.

The problem with this approach is that you get 1) a bad reputation with women; 2) relationships that end when women figure out you are lying; 3) a lot of pissed off people when they find out you are cheating.

Rather than messing with good woman's heads who just want to get married and have children, it is better to learn how to establish non-traditional relationships without lying.

A good friend of mine, who was a little older man at the time, told me when I was about 24 that the best lie was the truth. He explained that he used to lie and make up all kinds of stuff to get laid (all to no avail). Until one day he just got frustrated and started telling women the truth - that he was a liar and a cheater and had all kinds of mental problems and would make a very unreliable boyfriend and would probably sleep with other women -- and suddenly, he started getting laid left and right with no hassles.

I remembered his philosophy lesson and adopted it a year or two later when I got divorced and was on the market again. It worked.

Consequently, I used it ever since. And ever since that time I have had the ability to get typically four or five (but sometimes as many as ten) sexual partners without lying to or cheating on anyone. I do this when I am not in a committed relationship. And by-the-way, these are relationships I am talking about here, not one-niters. Some have gone on for as long as 5 years. But notice that I call them sexual partners and not "girlfriends" that is your first clue as I do not consider or represent any of them to be my girlfriend." Similarly, they do not represent me to be their boyfriend.

Now some guys like the idea of having sex with lots of women. I get men asking me particularly "How do you get a long term sexual relationship with a woman when you really don't want any more than that. How do you cut to the chase?"

I also get men asking me "How do you get multiple sexual relationships with women without lying to and cheating on them?"

So right here, right now I am going to answer those questions. Let's talk about how we establish relationships with three of the sexual categories that I talked about in my last article.

Lovers only
Multiple lovers
Arrangements

Now if you notice I picked out three categories to answer these questions because these are the kinds of relationships that you want (If you want to be honest and not lie, and not cheat on women.)

So the first step in establishing sexual (non-girlfriend) relationships and multiple sexual (non-girlfriend) relationships is to QUALIFY.

So it was the 70's when I got divorced and followed my friends advice, it was the era of free love and prior to aids. I was recently divorced, burnt out on the concept of marriage, had had a terrible married sex life and just wanted to have some fun for a few years before I got into a serious relationship again.

How did I qualify women? Well when I met women and they asked, the first thing I did was tell them just that. I told them exactly what was going on with me, and what I was looking for. I didn't sugar coat it to make it seem better or to trick some unsuspecting girl into having sex with me on the hopes of getting a boyfriend.

But there is more to it than that. There are certain types and kinds of women who are more likely to agree to be your lover and allow you to have multiple lovers. If you want these kinds of relationships than you need to be able to spot these kinds of women and go after them and not waste your time chasing after women who want boyfriends and husbands only.

Here are your prospects:

1) Career women. -- Women who are ambitious and career minded often do not want boyfriends. They consider boyfriends a distraction and a hindrance to their career. They do not have time to hang out with some guy every night. They ONLY want a lover to see once a week, twice a week or once every two weeks, etc. until they establish their careers.

2) Women looking for an arrangement. -- There are women who are looking for financial and/or emotional support from a man. They aren't looking for boyfriends as much as they are looking for HELP - a solution. If you talk to them they will usually make it known what they are looking for.

3) Women with integrity. -- Some women have a lot of integrity. They have high standards. They know what they want. And they know it is very hard to find. In the

meantime, they ONLY want a lover - preferably someone who is not needy or jealous and is perhaps busy and looking for a lover just like them.

4) Sexual women. -- Some women are super sexual and don't want to get tied down to one guy. They want to experience different men and to get to know them sexually as part of the overall experience.

5) Young women. -- Women 25 and younger aren't necessarily looking to get married. They are looking to understand men and themselves. They may want a boyfriend but they are also trying to learn and understand life. If you have something to offer, they just might spend a year or two of their life getting to know you.

6) Women who want to get to know you better first, before they get too involved. -- Doesn't matter if they say they don't want to have sex for a long time. What Matters is they don't want to get involved too quickly. They will spend time to get to know you. Being truthful might land you a mutually beneficial non-traditional relationship.

7) Women who are really into you. -- You know, you just meet this girl and she is totally into you and would do anything for you. Just tell her the truth. I once had a nurse friend who was totally into me. I told her the truth and she would cook me a great meal three times a week and then give me a great time in bed. Then she let me go out the other nights to have sex with other women with never a complaint.

8) A woman who likes you and needs or wants emotional or financial support from a man .(But is not necessarily seeking an arrangement from a man.) She is prime for an arrangement but she is just not thinking that way. So you are going to have to do the suggestions.

9) Women who aggressively want a boyfriend but can't find one because they are picky. They are usually picky because they are hot and guys approach them all wrong. Read the other sections of this book and these will be fairly easy to pick up.

10) Women who are recently divorced or having ended a relationship. Most of the time these women are NOT looking for a relationship for a while. However, they still get horny. When they are horny you will usually find them in a bar or club.

So what do you do if a woman fits into one of these categories? What if she doesn't?

If she doesn't fit into one of these categories, move on. You'll waste a lot of time trying to convert girls who want boyfriends and husbands over to your way of thinking. If she does fit into one of these categories, you must do the situational right thing for the personality.

Check out other things that I have written on my website as all dating and relationship technology applies all the time. Here I am just giving you the specifics of this situation.

So I won't go into everything about meeting and picking up women here that applies, but will focus on the aspects of establishing these kind of relationships.

Now if you look at the categories above they sort of break down into several major categories 1) women who really don't want a boyfriend right now or are too selective to realistically find one 2) women who want to be taken care of first and foremost 3) women who are really into you 4) women who are sexually curious

I have friends who ask me how I find so many women who will let me have multiple sex relationships. Well, it's easy if you select and qualify right. Now it does not mean that every woman in the above groupings is going to work out, but if you concentrate on the above groupings you are about 100 times more likely to find women who will be your lover or allow you multiple relationships than if you concentrate on the general population.

Now personally, when I approach a new woman prospect, I am actually not looking for these kinds of relationships. I actually want to get married again and that is what I am looking for. But as a man, I would fit in category three above. I'm too selective to find a girlfriend. I am looking for the perfect person and I am willing to wait. In the meantime, however, I want to have fun and I want to learn more about women and myself.

So when I approach a new woman I approach with the attitude that she probably won't be the perfect woman, but if she is it will take me a while (6 months at least) to get to know her but even if she isn't perfect I could have some fun with her while I'm getting to know her.

Now that's my attitude and it works for establishing lovers and multiple relationships.

I'm not in awe of women no matter how beautiful they are because ultimately it is the personality that is the elusive factor that makes a woman perfect for me. I've met thousands of women who are physically beautiful enough for me to marry, but now that I fully know what I want, I haven't met one with the right personality, interests, and compatibility factors that I would want to marry yet.

So, when I approach a woman I am not too serious about having to have a relationship with her. It is no big deal if it doesn't work out, I just enjoy the date that I am on. About 9 out of 10 women that I go out with want a second date with me, but I only go out with about 1 out of 10 women that I meet on a second date because of my own interest level.

During that first date, or first telephone call, etc. is when I do some heavy qualifying and set up for a multiple relationships if I am interested in the girl. I always qualify and set up any girl I meet in the above categories for multiple relationships. If she turns out to be the right girl you can always go from multiple relationships to a monogamous relationship very easily.

However, going from a monogamous relationship to multiple relationships is usually not possible and it would usually involve cheating on the first girl, which I personally have never been into.

Now my first and probably most important rule is if a woman does not ask me what I am looking for, I don't tell her. I focus on being romantic and seductive rather than talking about what kind of relationship I am looking for. If a woman does not bring up the subject it also tells me something about her - that she is not all that concerned and more than likely looking for something similar to what I am looking for.

There is also a certain type of woman who it is easier to set up multiple relationships with if you do it after you have had sex with her. Especially if you are a good lover, you can sometimes end up with a relationship with a woman who allows you, multiple relationships who wouldn't have if the conversation had come up prior to having sex. She would have disqualified herself by saying she is only looking for a monogamous relationship.

But after you have had sex with her, and the conversation comes up, and you tell her where you are at with it all, she now has a choice. She can keep you as a lover only - you are pleasant, romantic, and good in bed - while she either continues to look for her own marriage partner or get to know you better to see if it will work out between you two in time -- or she can let you go because she doesn't believe in multiple relationships.

Most women give it some time to see how it will work out between the two of you and grant you the freedom to do what you want as they realize they have that freedom too.

If the woman is one of the career minded ones, she may actually feel you are a very good match as she is too busy to see you more than once a week or so. Women don't like guys who sleep around a lot because of aids and other things like that, but in my case that is not what I am doing, I have long term relationships with women and I can tell the woman I meet about my other relationships if they want to know (usually they don't).

Occasionally women I have been with for over a year might suddenly ask me if I am sleeping with anyone else, and when I say yes, they sometimes tell me that they don't want to know in the future and to lie to them if they ask. Although it is not my policy to lie, I will respect a person's wishes and lie to them if they have requested it. I have learned over many years it is usually best to do what people ask you to do. Most people seem to know what is best for them.

Now when women bring up "what are you looking for" in these early date discussions, I talk about it fully and honestly. A crucial point to make to a woman is that you are not in a hurry to get married, or have a girlfriend or have sex. And that you are not jealous and you don't mind if a woman dates other guys when you are first starting to date her.

IF you have qualified the women properly, all of the types of women I have outlined above usually like this attitude as they are not looking for needy or jealous or possessive men, which the attitude above pretty much disclaims.

And honestly, when you can get all the women you want, you end up not being jealous or possessive or needy. Several of my long term multiple lover relationships were proceeded by three months or so of dating without sexual intercourse.

When a woman asks me point-blank what I am looking for off-the-bat I usually say what is true for me. Something like: "Well, ultimately, I am looking to get married again, but I am in no hurry. I believe it takes a little while really to get to know someone. And honestly, I am more than a little picky. So even though I ultimately want to get married again, knowing how picky I am for that, I also find myself wanting to just make friends and have some fun type relationships."

Now this statement leaves the door pretty much open for anything. I don't like saying it as it is a little too broad, but it is the truth. But I much prefer to be the first one to ask "What are you looking for?" if I see that she is going in that direction with her questions.

That way I can narrow down my response. If she is just looking for a lover or something, then I would drop off the marriage part and just say something like "I'm just looking for some fun right now as I am really busy and don't have time for a real boyfriend/girlfriend relationship.

Most of the girls in the above categories when asked will usually say something like they are just looking for a little fun or male companionship, nothing too serious, but if it eventually leads somewhere that is ok too.

Women tend to be a little more naturally monogamous than men. So often the women who allow me to have multiple relationships are themselves still monogamous with me.

Now with women who are looking for arrangements, it is quite simple. Let them make a proposition to you and if it is something you are interested in negotiate it. Not all arrangements are financial. I've had a working arrangement when I was 28 with a woman who was just tired of dating like I was. We both knew we would never get married but we made an arrangement to live together for two years and to help each other accomplish each other's goals. In the meantime, we lived together as girlfriend/boyfriend in a monogamous relationship so that we didn't have to be bothered with dating.

ARRANGEMENTS can be practical solutions to mutual problems or they can be out-and-out prostitution the same as a massage parlor can deliver legitimate massages or be a cover for prostitution.

For me a girl that will go to bed with ANYONE who gives her money is a prostitute no matter what she calls it. A woman who would marry ANY man she met that had a lot of money would still be a prostitute by my definition. On the other hand, a woman who limits her dating to guys that she likes who can also solve a few problems is simply being smart.

I once went out with beautiful actress who was pressing me hard for a relationship. She only liked going out with older guys who were emotionally and financially stable. When I asked her why, she said, "Why should I go out with some other actor who has the exact same problems as me and nothing to offer but good looks. I'd rather go out with someone who has something to offer me, to help me, and I something to offer them that they will appreciate and respect. It's a better fit"

Arrangements are fairly easy to accomplish if you are interested in such a relationship. The same groups of women you are prospecting for "lovers" and "multiple lovers" would be your prospects for arrangement. There are several ways of going about setting up arrangements.

1) If you date a lot of women, occasionally some of them will make a proposal to you. The first time it happened to me is was shortly after I started my "700 dates in a year." campaign. (See:"**How I Got 700 Dates in One Year**")
(http://datingtorelating.com/inc/sdetail/230)

One of the most beautiful women I had ever seen answered my ad. We got along fabulously on the phone and when we met, she told me she was having tremendous financial problems and was looking for a boyfriend who could at least help her with her rent. I couldn't at the time, but I sure wish I could have. Shortly thereafter, I found out there were many women looking for the same type of thing. If you date or meet a lot of women you will run into it sooner or later.

Honestly, though non-traditional, I find this group of women to be prettier and more honest than most women. How many times have you found yourself supporting a woman who covertly has you take her out to dinner all the time without giving you anything in return?

2) When you meet women and they tell you about all their problems they are having with men or life and you see a solution just propose it. (But first be romantic and seductive to get them really interested.) You have nothing to lose and sometimes it will be the clincher. Keep it out of prostitution. That is degrading for everyone. However, if you see a solution to her problem, if you have something to offer her that is non-traditionally discussed in boyfriend/girlfriend relationships go for it.

If, for example, when she tells you she never had an orgasm with her old boyfriend, and if you are a good lover suggest she ought to hook up with you for a while to learn about sex and experience some orgasms. If you both share the same fetish or fantasy, suggest hooking up just for that enjoyment once in awhile.

There is always an exchange factor in arrangements. A trade of something for something. But there is also a limiting factor in arrangements. Arrangements are usually not relationships that go on forever. There is usually some practical purpose that when achieved will end the relationship. However, I have known many people who started out with an arrangement and ended up with a traditional relationship.

There are plenty of people you have met and will meet who instantly know you are not the one for them. Or you know they are not the one for you. But sometimes these people have something to offer you, just not the complete package. Rather than waste them, communicate to them. There may be a learning experience or something rewarding in it for you.

3) There are hundreds of dating sites dedicated to alternative dating. If you want to work out an arrangement, these kinds of dating sites and dating ads are fertile grounds for prospecting. People are pretty upfront in these kinds of ads, but watch out for prostitutes who use alternative ads for cover. In other words there are women who have 7 different guys supporting them (one for each night of the week) and they do nothing else with their life but this. To me that is a prostitute.

How does SAFE SEX fit into multiple relationships?

Well first let me point out that multiple relationships is not the same thing as going out and getting laid by a different woman in a bar or club every night (which I have done too when I was younger and when it was the pre-aids era)

Having unprotected sex is not something I do at all unless I have had mutual aids tests and I know the person is monogamous with me. The people I select as sexual partners are also not leading a promiscuous life style. I wouldn't get involved with someone who was.

What I am doing is having relationships -not one-night stands - with several people at once. The same care and thought goes into selecting these sexual partners as one would put into selecting a monogamous sexual partner.

Even when I was younger and was getting laid by a different woman every night in the bars and clubs, I was still very careful on qualifying people and never caught any venereal diseases. Most often back then I qualified women by the length of time it had been since they broke up with their boyfriend. I usually only went out with women who hadn't had sex in about a year. I found these type of women to be fairly un-promiscuous and safe to have spontaneous sex with.

Most all of the women I select are actually monogamous with me. However, there comes a point after a while where the woman usually falls in love with me and wants to get married or exclusive or something. These are my friends so I have to handle the rejection of that kind of relationship delicately while maintaining a "lover" relationship. After I do so, however, the woman often start actively looking for a boyfriend or husband and they do have the freedom to try out someone else while we are still being lovers. This had happened to me a few times and the women have talked to me about it openly.

When they find someone else, we end our sexual relationship and I find someone to replace the lover.

So to recap, to establish non-traditional relationships such as arrangements, lovers or multiples lovers with honestly you need to qualify your prospects or you chances will be slim, and then you need to communicate openly and honestly what you are looking for.

It is a big world and there is always someone who is looking for the same thing you are. But no one will know it unless you communicate it.

Now after you have qualified a woman and you have established a relationship with her the same principles of creating a relationship that I talk about elsewhere apply. There is one additional rule however, that you have to remember when creating non-boyfriend/girlfriend relationships.

Don't call or see the woman more than 1 or 2 times a week. If you see her more than that, you will be acting like a boyfriend. If you act like a boyfriend, she will start assuming you are a boyfriend and start treating you like one and expecting you to act more like one. Jealousy, possessiveness, and other things like drama will start to set it. Suddenly she won't want you seeing other women

So if you want to keep a lover as a lover, an arrangement as an arrangement - create it, have fun with it, but keep a little distance - have a good pleasant time when you get together but don't do it too frequently or it will back fire on you.

12) HOW TO MAKE LOVE TO A WOMAN

Foreplay

A lot of guys think that foreplay is having to kiss your girlfriend or wife before she lets you have intercourse. Well a lot of guys think they are great lovers, but a lot of women have other thoughts about that.... I have different thoughts about foreplay.

Foreplay, what is that? Good question.

Foreplay is whatever creates a little sex flow between your girl and you and holds it there in place so she and you can think about it and enjoy the build up and anticipation of what is eventually to come.

Another way of saying it is that foreplay is what "gets you or your partner ready" for the sex act. Since guys are just about biologically ready for the sex act "all the time." Guys seem to forget the value of foreplay, after all, it is something they have to do for someone else -- not themselves.

Bad way of looking at it. Why? Foreplay is not just for established couples already having sex. Foreplay is what prepares a woman to have sex with you. Hence, any woman you would like to have sex with that you are NOT having sex with would require foreplay.

So foreplay has a role in meeting women, attracting women, picking up women, dating women, having a relationship with women, and making love to women.

Flirting is foreplay....

I got married at 22 to my first girlfriend, and though I had sex for 5 or 6 years before we got divorced. I never actually made love until after I broke up with and divorced my wife. Why? We were both pretty inexperienced. Looking back, we had plenty of sex, but hardly any foreplay. The first time I actually made love, I was seduced. And there were hours and hours of foreplay.

So after getting divorced, I stood around bars and clubs nightly for a month or two. But after a while I started learning a few things. Then I started having sex daily (one night standers) with different women. (This was the 70's -- free love -- pre-AIDS.) Man, did I get a lot of experience then. These women taught me stuff. Stuff, I didn't know, but now do.

One of the things I learned is that women like and need foreplay to enjoy sex. And apparently it made it a whole lot better for me too!

A Woman's, unlike a man's, sexual organ takes a while to physically respond to sexual stimuli and urges. Men can be ready in a minute, women take a little longer but mentally

I think men and women are more even. Foreplay can mentally prepare either sex in such a way to make the love making experience a whole lot better.

I feel that usually at least an hour of bedroom foreplay is a minimal amount of time to prepare a woman and myself both mentally and physically for the sex act.

However, foreplay can go on longer than that....

The best kind of foreplay is Romance....you know, shopping with your girl in the mall, holding hands as you walk, having a sexy conversation and flirtation at lunch. Little kisses and touches throughout the day. Getting so turned on that you both can't wait to go home.

Foreplay can go on for hours and hours and hours.

When you are in the bedroom foreplay is kissing and kissing and kissing, touching, touching and touching. It can be role-playing, talking about your fantasies, taking a bath or shower together, feeding each other, or watching sexy movies, or whatever other little sexy games you are into together. (If you are into that.)

So how do you know when it is the right time to end the foreplay and start in on the sex act itself? Well when you are young and stupid, you don't think about any one but yourself. You start kissing your girl and a minute later you have an erection. Two minutes later you have her clothes off and you are trying to stick it in. Why? Because your thought is "If I'm feeling it, she must be feeling it too. See she is kissing me passionately isn't she. She must be feeling it." But, when you try to put it in, it won't go, so she offers to get out the old lubricant. She does and 10 minutes later it is all over. "I didn't have an orgasm," she complains. "You want me to do something?" you ask, even though you are really no longer interested. "Never mind" she says.

It is a shame how many women out there have never been made love to properly. It is amazing how many women think that lubricant is normal, have never had a vaginal orgasm, or have never experienced multiple orgasms.

MEN, good sex for women starts with FOREPLAY. Consider this your call to duty!

So, here are some basic principles for guys in relationships.

1) Always devote at least an hour to foreplay when you are in the bedroom. And use romance as foreplay throughout the week, days, and hours leading up to the bedroom. Women like to talk. Talking (and you listening) can be a very sexy foreplay for a woman.

2) Never, never, never, try to have intercourse with a woman until her private parts are soaking wet with anticipation. If she is not wet, she is not ready. She needs more foreplay. (Actually even if she is soaking wet, she probably still wants more.)

3) Always, always, always make sure your girl has an orgasm before you do. Why? Because it is no fun having sex with someone who only takes care of themselves and then is too tired to do anything about you. If your girl has multiple orgasms then she might need to orgasm two, three or four times before you do. If you don't know what multiple orgasms are then try some more foreplay and look up "tantra technique" on the internet. Not all women have multiple orgasms, but if you do your part right, most are capable of it.

Now these are generalizations, there are exceptions to the things I have written here. (For example, there is a small percentage of women who always need lubricant because of a medical condition.) But, if you know anything about my philosophy, from my other in depth writing, you know I am totally into situational technique. But the above is fairly consistent for about 80% of women I've experienced.

How to Get Your Wife or Girlfriend to Want More Sex

The biggest complaint that guys in relationships have, is not getting enough sex from their wife or girlfriend.

In a recent AskMen.com poll 44% of men said, (when asked about their overall sex life) "I wish I had sex more frequently".

On our website, DatingToRelating.com, in a poll of single men "How to Get Your Wife Or Girlfriend To Want More Sex" and "How To Get Sex More Often" were two of the books single men were most interested in reading.

Guys I've talked to sometimes think that women just aren't as sexual or into sex as much as guys.

My experience, however, has been to the contrary. Women are by far MORE sexual and enjoy sex much more than men do. Their orgasms typically last longer and as a group they are much more capable of multiple orgasms than men.

Yet, is very typical to hear a married guy complain that he only gets sex from his wife or girlfriend once a month. And of course it has been the subject of many a comedy on TV and in the movies.

So why is it if women are more sexual then men that men are the ones who are usually complaining about not getting enough sex.

The answer lies in two differences between men and women.

1) Women don't get physically turned on as easily as men. And conversely women get turned off more easily than men. So if I guy is not doing or saying the right things to his girl, she won't get turned on, and in fact might get turned off.

2) Combine that with the fact that women have one ability that men don't have and you will start to get a better understanding of the situation -- Even though women are more sexual and enjoy sex more deeply than men are capable of, women are also capable of going without sex for longer periods of time. Women are not as sexually "needy" as men.

Let's put it another way - Sex is first and foremost a "quality" thing for women.

Look at some of the women's complaint's in polls:

> 90% of women reported that they wished their partner kissed them more or with more passion.
>
> 65% of women felt their partner did not have a good kissing technique. So, you see, men are more into quantity and women are more into quality.

But, here is what you should know, if you give a woman the "quality" of sexual relations that she is desiring then she will want the quantity. And when you really turn your woman on, and she is in the quality and quantity mode. Most women will have most men on the mat screaming "No Mas" in a short period of time.

So if your woman is not having sex with you as frequently as you'd like, then you can safely assume that you are not doing something right in the "quality" department. You are either turning her off or not turning her on - in any case, you are doing something wrong.

Now, what do guys do wrong to mess up the frequency of their sex life. Well there are probably 100s of answers to that one and millions of unique variations on the theme. But, here are some of the more basic and frequent mistakes that men make in their relationships with women.

First let's look at what guys can do to turn women off.

1) Being a slob, smelly, or physically disgusting. - I don't think I have to go into this too much, but if you want sex, you might try approaching your woman when you are fresh and clean, rather than dirty and smelly. If you like to have sex when you go to bed at night, try taking a shower first. Make sure she knows you are doing that, then get romantic.

2) Not taking care of your responsibilities as a man. - Most often, it is not about being dirty and smelly but about not doing your job as a man. Men are supposed to support a family. They are supposed to take care of women. Although women are liberated these days and work and earn money like men, that doesn't mean that having to work and support a family turns them on. Most women are ok with contributing to the support of the family unit or boyfriend/girlfriend team, but when they start contributing more than the man and the man is plainly not doing his fair share because he is lazy or some such other trait, that's when women get a little turned off and resentful.

Almost every time I go out to a nice restaurant and I see a young couple paying for the meal, it is most often the woman that pays. What is that about? I can tell the difference between married couples and dating singles. Guys may think they are cool because their woman will pay for them everywhere they go, and they may even get normal sex for awhile, but I guarantee you women eventually get turned off by this kind of thing, especially when one of the girlfriends starts bragging about how well her husband or boyfriend is doing and how he does all these nice things for her.

Women can even tolerate a guy who isn't too bright and is trying as hard as he can. Women will even at times get fooled when they are young into thinking a guy has potential when he doesn't -- and thus they invest and give their all to the "rock star guitarist" who is trying to make his career. But that get's old after a while and after 2 or 3 years of that, women get turned off and resentful for supporting a man who is going nowhere. Women don't mind an equal partner, but they certainly do mind a guy who is just not being a man and taking on the responsibilities of "manhood" or making things go right in his own career.

3) Sometimes, it is not about career and the responsibilities of manhood, but about equality of effort and fair exchange amongst group members. So when the guy and the woman both have jobs and the guy is holding his own and even making a little more than the woman, that is all good except when they both come home and she is expected to clean up the house and do his laundry while he sits around lazily and drinks beer.

You see, all of the above scenarios are mood killers for women. Even though women may tolerate some of these behaviors at first, in a long-term relationship these kind of behaviors eventually catch up with her and start killing the mood.

4) On top of that is communication. Because of the above perceived inequities women will start "bitching' at men about their career or their responsibilities or their chores at home, etc. When men are unresponsive to communication, to discussing and handling the complaints, etc. there is only one direction for the communication to go - less sex. She is not turned on. She can't change anything about it with communication, so she just becomes not interested in sex.. Some women may even consciously withhold sex on purpose to get across to you that "something is wrong" and that "we need to talk."

When a guy still doesn't get what this "lack of sexual interest" is really about, the relationship becomes doomed to one of mediocrity or eventual breakup.

I think the majority of "lack of sexual interest" exhibited by women are the result of the above perceived inequities - which really just turn women off sexually.

Occasionally however, it is not because of the above, it is because of a failure to turn women on properly, that sexual interest is lost.

Most commonly, it is actually both things at once, because most men who are turning women off are simultaneously failing to turn them on. So most guys who are not getting sex often enough need to work both on turning women on as well as not turning women off. However, occasionally there are guys who are not turning women off, they just aren't doing a very good job at turning women on. That is an easier case to handle.

What mistakes do guys make in regards to turning women on? Here are the four most common mistakes that I find men making with respect to turning women on.

1) No Romance - Now I've talked about this one extensively in my other writings. So let me just put it simply here. You can't stop romancing a girl after you get her to be your girlfriend or wife. Whatever you did to get the girl, you have to keep doing it, do it more extensively, find new ways of doing it, etc. - as long as you want to keep creating a relationship with this person, you have to keep creating romance with them.

2) Boring Sexual Routine - Sometimes people fall into a sexual routine that is fun a first put becomes boring when done day after day, night after night. Try some new things. Vary the routine. It will help keep things fresh and interesting between the two of you. Talk about your likes, desires, and new things you would like to try. Talk about your fantasies. Be willing to do things she would like to do in exchange for trying things you would like to do. If you run out of ideas, we have a free mini-courses on our website, "How To Be a Great Lover" and other free materials to help you out with ideas.

3) Not understanding a woman's body - a lot of guys, especially the younger ones, don't understand a woman's body. Women need more preparatory (before actual sex) stimulation than men. Men only have to think about it and seem to be ready to do the deed. Women need to think about it and think about it and think about it to become interested and turned on.

Extensive foreplay is a necessity for women to get physically ready and mentally ready to enjoy and get into sex. Talking, having a romantic dinner, holding hands, kissing for hours (like you did on your first dates) all prepares a woman's body for sex and turns her on. Never, never, never try to have intercourse with a woman until she is turned on. Keep kissing, keep touching, but never have intercourse until she is totally turned on.

How do you know when she is totally turned on? Well, she will be soaking wet and she won't need any lubricant. Lubricant was invented because guys don't know how or don't take the time to turn a woman on. When you turn a woman on, you won't ever need lubricant.

4) Not taking a woman to multiple orgasms. - Practically any woman is capable of multiple orgasms. Many think they aren't so they don't try and many aren't turned on enough or are a little turned off by their lover so that prevents them from having multiple orgasms.

The reality though is practically all women can have multiple orgasms. Some need some time between orgasm, while others are little orgasmic machines that can continue having orgasm after orgasm for hours on end. The ability to orgasm and to have multiple orgasm can be developed in women who think they are incapable by a knowledgeable man.

This is a subject that books are written on and if you don't know how to make a woman orgasm than I suggest you get one and learn how to make a woman orgasm. (See "**How To Give Any Woman Orgasms**" (http://datingtorelating.com/inc/sdetail/3379) on our website.)

Making a woman multiple orgasm is similar. You need to learn to observe your partner's body. Learn and understand how it works. Some men are even unsure if a woman is even having an orgasm.

If you are observant you will start to observe and know when she is having an orgasm. Sometimes you can feel the orgasm tighten around you as you are having sex, other times you can feel the woman's whole body tighten as she begins to orgasm, sometimes there is quiver or a vibration from her as she begins to orgasm, other times she begins to get vocal as she orgasms, or the opposite, she becomes silent as she begins to orgasm

Each woman is uniquely different from my experiences, but any woman can be figured out if you just become observant.

Sometimes a woman's vagina gets sore or dry after the first orgasm and you need to withdraw from sexual intercourse after she orgasms and go back to light foreplay, building the foreplay up again into another orgasm later. Other women stay lubricated after the first orgasm and you can just continue having sex and the woman will orgasm over and over again.

As I have said, women are uniquely different and you will just need to observe your partner and figure out how to get her to multiple orgasm. As a general principle however, whenever it hurts her, back off of intercourse and go back to foreplay. Never have intercourse until she is naturally wet.

For some women multiple orgasms are achieved outside of intercourse. My last girlfriend liked to have the first orgasm by finger or hand, the second by mouth, and the third and subsequent orgasms by intercourse.

This may work well for a woman who becomes dry or irritated by intercourse after her first orgasm, but you can also do the reverse in that case, depending on the woman -- first orgasm by intercourse then second or third orgasm by mouth or hand.

For some women, orgasms are always achieved outside of intercourse. Sometimes two bodies just don't fit together the right way to naturally create an orgasm for the woman. Be willing to give your partner an orgasm each time you have sex, any way you can - by finger or hand, by mouth, or by machine if you have to.

Please your partner. Do whatever it takes. Always think of her and her pleasure first.
As a rule I always give my partner her orgasm or orgasms first before I orgasm as it is much harder (both physically and mentally) to give your partner an orgasm when you are flaccid.

If you learn to make a woman orgasm and multiple orgasm each time you have sex with her and you don't do the big mistakes to turn her off up above, I guarantee you she will give you all the sex you want.

I've even had relationships in which we totally did not get along, but the sex was so good for her, that she could not break up with me, and even after we did break up, she would keep coming back for sex.

In conclusion, if you learn to 1) NOT do the things that turn women off, and 2) do the things that turn women on, you will probably get more sex out of your woman than you can handle. Then I will have to answer your questions when you write to me like this:

> "My girl and I really have fantastic sex, and I really love her, but please, she is wearing me out, I can't keep up with her demands for sex. What do I do to slow her down, without offending her?"

Male Sexual Dysfunction and Relationships

Every guy has times when things don't quite work the way they are supposed to down in his "love department."

When I was a young man it would happen oh….. once every blue moon or so. However, I never paid much attention to it. If something did not work, I would just back off sex for a few days, and then everything would be back to normal.

In my late twenties I experienced my first bout of extended male dysfunction – you know, it does not work for a week or so. I had a girlfriend who was putting a lot of pressure on me in the relationship department. We had agreed to a "convenience" relationship but she was falling in love with me and putting pressure on me to take our relationship in a direction I did not want to go.

After a while things started to "not work properly" down there and she took it personal. I told her it had nothing to do with my attraction to her. I explained to her that it was just an emotional reaction to the pressure she was putting on me. She backed off the pressure, and we refrained from lovemaking for about a week and everything went back to normal.

I learned a valuable lesson, however. I learned that my "love department" was very sensitive to emotional pressure.

I guess I never looked at male dysfunction as a problem. It was just something that happened every once in a while and it seemed to be related to my emotions more than anything else.

I went through a couple of marriages and divorces and long-term relationships and break ups and I noticed the same thing. Towards the end of a relationship, when things were not going that good emotionally, my "love department" and my libido seemed to be low in performance and attitude, respectively.

The solution was always the same. Back off of sex for a week or two, and things always went back to normal. (I innately knew that what I did not want to do was to keep "forcing" the issue and making myself feel bad for my lack of performance. By backing off sex for a week or so, I would just get so horny that it always worked without fail.)

When I got into my 50s and I was single again, I fell into a unique perspective on sexual dysfunction. You know, by the time you start hitting 50 or so things are not suppose to work as well as they use to due to aging and other physical realities.

However, the following incident made me wonder just how much of what we attribute to aging and physical factors may not actually be so.

Now if you have been following my writings you know that I am an advocate of multiple dating as well as an advocate of monogamy. I have multiple relationships when I am not in a committed relationship. And I am completely monogamous when I am in a committed relationship.

I was dating five or six lovely young women after I ended a long-term relationship around age 50. One night on a "first romantic encounter" with this new lovely young woman I met, my "love department" totally failed on me. I could not get it interested in doing its job.

The next night I saw one of my regular girls and surprisingly everything was fine. No problem at all. Everything was also fine for a few more dates with the other women I was seeing until I circled back to the new young lovely woman. Suddenly, my "love department" did not want to do its job again.

Just about this time, I met another young woman and brought her into the fold. I had the same problem with this second new young woman that I was having with the first.

However, when I went back to my regulars there was no problem at all.

I quickly figured out that there had to be something going on emotionally with these two new young women that I was obviously reacting to. It was obviously not physical but a mental reaction that I was having.

I began to wonder, though. What if I was a regular guy and only dating one woman. Moreover, what if that one woman was one of these two girls? Being 50 and all I would definitely have begun to think there was something physical going on and that I was losing it due to age. However, if I had thought that I would actually have been totally wrong – barking up the wrong tree.

I would have probably started on Viagra or something, been constantly worried about my performance, and generally felt bad about my love life. Instead, because I just happened to be multiple dating at this time of my life, I knew for a fact that this was some sort of emotional reaction and nothing physical at all.

How many 50-plus year old men out there have an emotional upset and think it is due to aging or some other physical factor? I bet quite a few.

Well the emotional aspect of these relationships was the right tree to bark up, and I confronted what was actually emotionally upsetting me with each of these girls. One was practically a virgin and did not really know what to do. She was 25 or so, so I didn't expect that and I was reading all her signals wrong. When she finally confessed to her lack of experience, I started teaching her what to do and she eventually turned into one of the best lovers I ever had. She was a very sensual girl, just a little inexperienced.

The other girl just had a personality that did not quite match up with mine. She was one of those kinds of girls that want the man to do everything – make all the decisions, make all the moves, etc. Personally, I like a little more give and take than that in a relationship.

But as we got to know and understand each other better we both compromised a little and she likewise turned into a very good lover.

In both cases, it took three or four months of working at it to develop a good physical relationship, but not only did I NOT feel bad about myself, I got to know two women that I probably wouldn't have gotten to know if it weren't for my unique situation. If I had been practicing monogamy, I would have given up on both of these women very quickly – writing them off as romantically incompatible.

I always thought a couple had to hit it off quickly in the lovemaking department or it just wasn't going to work. These two experiences opened up my mind to other possibilities.

So, there are actually a couple of points I am trying to make here.

1) If you feel like you have male dysfunction, why don't you look at your relationship first before you decide that it is purely physical and start taking drugs. All my life I had pretty much associated male dysfunction with emotional issues, but nothing made it so clear as my recent experiences.

2) Emotional male dysfunction is not a bad thing. It is just your body communicating to you that something is wrong, that you are upset about something. Rather than blowing off the person and situation involved, if you really like the person, find out what is behind the emotional reaction. Two of the very best lovers I ever had came out of confronting my male dysfunction with them and working through it. In the end it was definitely worth it.

Sexual Technique - How to Make Love to a Woman

On our website, we have detailed information on sexual technique. We even have mini-courses like: "**How To Be A Great Lover**" "**How To Be A Great Kisser"** and "**Everything You Ever Wanted To Know About Sex Positions**." (http://datingtorelating.com/inc/sdetail/3395)

Sexual technique is again a topic worthy of a book and indeed many a book has been written on the subject.

But here I am going to give you some general pointers and an example. The example contains some basic principles even more basic then the techniques we have on the website.

Lovemaking is sensuality. It involves the whole body not just genitals.

Pre – Session

1) Foreplay – apply what I have told you in Chapter 12(a). Foreplay begins way before the sex act and the love making session. Flirt with your woman all day and both of you will be real turned on when you are ready to engage.

2) Sobriety – I was 28 before I ever made love sober. Making love sober is a must. Alcohol makes a man slightly flaccid. If you don't believe me. Try it. Make love to your woman sober and inebriated. Ask her which one she likes best. If everything else is equal she will always pick sober over inebriated. Why? Because she will tell you, you are a lot harder when you are sober.

3) Cleanliness- Having been with a lot of women, it makes a big difference when someone is clean and smells nice. Keep your hygiene in. Take a shower; clean your teeth; use deodorant, gargle, etc.

Example of a sensual love making session your woman will enjoy.

1) Foreplay – now this is direct sexual foreplay - kissing, touching, petting, etc. You have to do foreplay for at least an hour. Touch, kiss, and caress her entire body – not just the genitals. Women have many erogenous zones in addition to their breasts and their clitoris – Lips, scalp, hair, ears, neck, inner thighs, butt, and the back.

2) Every woman is different but I work may way up the erogenous zones. Start off with kissing the lips lightly and gently, work into making out with deep French kissing, massage the scalp and play with the hair while you are kissing her. Use your hands while kissing to tantalize her whole body. Play with her hands, her toes, lightly stroke her arms, her back. Withdraw from French kissing

after doing it for a while (30-60 minutes) and begin to kiss her entire body with her clothes on. Talk to her occasionally as you kiss her. Whisper sweat nothings in her ear. Tell her how much you love her. Tell her how beautiful she is to you. (Keep the light talking going throughout your love making session.) Kiss her neck, her shoulders, pull her top down over her shoulder to kiss her shoulders, its sexy and she'll like it. Lift her top up to kiss her stomach. Move all over her body kiss her legs, her thighs, kiss her shins and her feet. Roll her over and kiss the back of her neck, her back, her buttocks, her legs, etc.

3) Now begin to undress her as you kiss her. Open her blouse and kiss her all over her chest and her stomach. Kiss her on her bra, pull her bra strap off her shoulder and kiss her shoulders. Pull her bra down a little and kiss the top of her breasts, pull it down a little more and lick her nipples, pop her breasts out o her bra cup and suck her nipples. After a while place her breast back in her bra and move to another spot. If she is wearing pants undue her zipper, pull her pants open slightly around the zipper and kiss her around her waistline and her pubic area. Kiss her legs with her pants on. Kiss her between the legs with her pants on. If she is wearing a dress or a skirt, lift her skirt up and kiss her legs and thighs, kiss her waistline and her pubic area, kiss her between her legs. – Then move down to her feet kissing every part of her body all the while.

4) Flip her over. Kiss the back of her neck, lift her shirt up, and kiss her back. Now undo her bra and kiss her back some more. Kiss her butt with her panties on. After a while, if she is wearing pants now it is time to take them off. Roll her over, and pull them off of her. If she is wearing a skirt take her panties off, but leave her skirt on. Now it is time to start giving her some oral sex. Reach and withdraw. Give her some oral sex, and then go back to some French kissing, now humping her with your body as you kiss her. Kiss and suck on her breasts again. If she has multiple orgasms now is the time to give her, her first orgasm. Give her oral sex while using your finger to massage her g-spot at the same time. If she is a single orgasm woman, turn her on with oral sex, but withdraw before she comes.

5) Now it is time to take all her clothes off and remove yours. Make sure she is still wet, go back to French kissing and kissing her all over her body while playing with her vagina and clitoris with your finger. Suck her breasts again. Lick her breasts and her stomach - Make sure her vagina is soaking wet before you enter. Now it is time to enter. (I won't go into positions – see "**Everything You Ever Wanted To Know About Sex Positions**." (http://datingtorelating.com/inc/sdetail/3395) for that - as positions will be varied from time to time depending on your mood and the girl – different people fit better in different ways.)

6) Enter slowly, caress her close to you, hug her, hold her. Do not enter all the way at first. Use short slow strokes and only insert an inch or so then withdraw. Set up a rhythm. Slowly enter deeper, working your way up to full deep thrusts over time.

7) Pay attention to her body signals. Women come in different ways. Some get tight and hard all over when they are getting ready to come. Others get aggressive and change into a position that is easy for them to come in with you. Other get vocal, others start sweating. Everyone is different. Know your woman and know her signals.

8) Know your timing. Are you trying to make love for hours or all night, or all you trying to give each of you an orgasm and then end your session. Or are you trying to give her (or both of you) multiple orgasms and then call it a night. If intending to go a long time or all night, reach and withdraw from the orgasm point, so as to not quite have an orgasm until you are ready to end. If you are trying to give her (or you) multiple orgasms then depending on how she has her multiple orgasms you may need to simply keep yourself from coming until she has her orgasms. (See "**How To Make Sex Last Longer**" http://datingtorelating.com/inc/sdetail/3378) or you may give her (or you) an orgasm then withdraw from sex for a while talking or playing while hugging or caressing until ready to start again. Or you may simply revert to Afterplay until she is wet and you are hard again (See Afterplay below).

9) Afterplay – Don't end your love making on an orgasm. Follow through. Show her you love her and it is not just about sex and orgasms. Wind down with some foreplay which is now called afterplay. Kissing, hugging, kissing all over, touching, caressing, kissing. End with kissing. If you are working on multiple orgasms, afterplay can turn into foreplay and set you up for another lovemaking session. But even after multiple orgasms and multiple love-making sessions you will always end the whole thing with afterplay.

That is a sample of how to make love to a woman. Of course, it is done spontaneously. It is not to be memorized like a zombie or done exactly the same each time. In order to keep a relationship fresh, you have to avoid routine and habit and try new and varied techniques. But the things each of your love making sessions should always have in common are:

1) Sensuality
2) Lots of foreplay and after play
3) Use your whole body and make love to your partners whole body.
4) Lots of kissing.
5) Observation – get to know your partner's body and how it works.
6) Communicate – talk to her as you make love. Say sweat nothings as well as finding out what feels good and what doesn't. (Also, talk to her about sex, when you are not having sex. It is pre-session foreplay and it is a way of finding out what is needed or wanted.

SUMMARY

Well you have been given a technology for dating and a technology for relating.

You have been given many situational strategies for both dating and relating.

Use the strategies for short-term immediate effects. Use the technologies to create long-term stable effects and more short-term situational strategies.

If you have questions post them on any of our various blogs or forums, or email your questions to info@DatingToRelating.com. We can't answer all questions personally, but we will post answers to frequently asked questions on our website or send you an email with the answers to questions a lot of guys have been asking.

Wishing you success…

For more books on the subjects of DATING and RELATING visit our PRODUCTS PAGE at http://datingtorelating.com/products

Mr. L. Rx

APPENDIX

Other DATING and RELATING products from www.DatingToRelating.com.

Phone Consultations with Mr. L. Rx Now Available!

Go to: **http://datingtorelating.com/services**

Private Phone Consultation
Price:$1,000.00/ per Hour

If you would like your own private consultation with Mr. L. Rx go to: **http://datingtorelating.com/services**
Please leave your name and contact information and indicate what topic you would like your consultation to cover in the comments.

How To Make Sex Last Longer - by Dr. Dating
http://datingtorelating.com/inc/sdetail/3378
Reg. Price: ~~$20.00~~
Sale Price: $7.00
Save: $13.00

SPECIAL OFFER

HOW TO MAKE SEX LAST LONGER - $ 7.00

** NEW 2007 Version **

How To Make Sex Last Longer

Many sexually active males would like to "keep it up" longer - until their woman is fully satisfied and for their own more fulfilling, long lasting pleasure. Since it's no secret that it takes women longer to climax, guys need to delay their ejaculation if they really want to satisfy their partner. Everyone knows that longer intercourse is much more satisfying than "quickies" for both parties. Thanks to Dr. Dating, the secret is out - everyone can easily lengthen their lovemaking just by applying the techniques from Dr. Dating's latest eBook, *How to Make Sex Last Longer*.

How To Give Any Woman an Orgasm - by Dr. Dating
http://datingtorelating.com/inc/sdetail/3379
Reg. Price: ~~$20.00~~
Sale Price: $7.00
Save: $13.00

HOW TO GIVE ANY WOMAN ORGASMS - $7.00

**** NEW 2007 Version ****

How To Give Any Woman Orgasms

The female body is a mystery to most men - even to those who have had thousands of sexual conquests. What is it that makes women tick? What do women really want in bed? These questions may have perplexed you for so long, and you're not alone. Finally, Dr. Dating has written a complete, tried and tested guide on *How to Give Any Woman Orgasms*.

How to make Sex Last Longer - Special Love Package
http://datingtorelating.com/inc/sdetail/3395

Reg. Price: ~~$100.00~~
Sale Price: $14.00
Save: $86.00

NEW ARRIVAL

SPECIAL OFFER!

Buy HOW TO MAKE SEX LAST LONGER and HOW TO GIVE ANY WOMAN ORGASMS - $14.00

and get THREE FREE compilation eBooks FROM Mr. L. Rx

EVERYTHING YOU WANTED TO KNOW ABOUT SEX POSITIONS

HOW TO BE A GREAT LOVER

HOW TO BE A GREAT KISSER

How To Be Successful with Women - by Dr. Dating

http://datingtorelating.com/inc/sdetail/3380

Reg. Price: ~~$20.00~~
Sale Price: $7.00
Save: $13.00

SPECIAL OFFER

HOW TO BE SUCCESSFUL WITH WOMEN - $7.00

** NEW 2007 Version **

How To Be Successful With Women

Ever thrown your arms up in the air, confused about something a woman said or did? You're not alone! Most men don't have an answer to the question of "What do women want?" Most men, that is, except for Dr. Dating. In his eBook "How to Be Successful with Women," Dr. Dating tackles the complexities of the female mind, and he's written it for YOU! He's handing you nothing short of the keys to the kingdom.

The Art of Conversation - by Dr. Dating
http://datingtorelating.com/inc/sdetail/3381

Reg. Price: ~~$20.00~~
Sale Price: $7.00
Save: $13.00

SPECIAL OFFER

THE ART OF CONVERSATION - $ 7.00

**** Published 2006 ****

The Art Of Conversation
We've all been there - the non-stop sweating and stuttering slowly becomes an embarrassment because you're simply too nervous to talk to the object of your attraction. Whether you're a sensitive guy or a sassy girl, you probably still get tongue-tied during parties, first dates, or even a simple conversation in your office lounge. Not to worry - Dr. Dating has created just the thing that can help you get your tongue out of a twist.

The Beginners Guide To Virtual Sex - by Dr. Dating
http://datingtorelating.com/inc/sdetail/3384
Reg. Price: ~~$20.00~~
Sale Price: $7.00
Save: $13.00

SPECIAL OFFER

THE BEGINNERS GUIDE TO VIRTUAL SEX - $ 7.00

The Beginners Guide to Virtual Sex

It doesn't matter if you're a virgin or promiscuous, single or in a committed relationship - ABSOLUTELY ANYONE can have fulfilling, pleasurable sex in the virtual world. All you need is a phone line or an internet connection. This guide will show you EVERYTHING you need to know about mastering the world of virtual sex.

** Published 2007 **

How To Find A Fk Buddy - by Dr. Dating**
http://datingtorelating.com/inc/sdetail/3383
Reg. Price: ~~$20.00~~
Sale Price: $7.00
Save: $13.00

SPECIAL OFFER

HOW TO FIND A F**K BUDDY - $7.00

How To Find A Fk Buddy**

If you think it's impossible to list "sex" as a recreational activity, you're wrong! Whether you're as suave as James Bond or as ordinary as the Average Joe, you need to know the secrets of finding your own special "friend with benefits". Having a fk buddy can be a sensual adventure unlike any other and you deserve to be on that adventure! This guide can give you tried and tested methods that will help you get the f**k buddy**

**** Published 2007 ****

Coping With A Small Penis - by Dr. Dating

http://datingtorelating.com/inc/sdetail/3382

Reg. Price: ~~$20.00~~
Sale Price: $7.00
Save: $13.00

SPECIAL OFFER

COPING WITH A SMALL PENIS - $7.00

** NEW 2007 Version **

Coping With A Small Penis

This eBook is an inspiring story about how a young man copes with a small penis - and uses this "lack of size" as an advantage. It's no secret that most men worry about whether they are "big enough" to please a woman, and this story will definitely make you feel better about the size of your own penis, as well as your masculinity.

Dealing With Loneliness - by SideKick
http://datingtorelating.com/inc/sdetail/3387
Reg. Price: ~~$20.00~~
Sale Price: $7.00
Save: $13.00

SPECIAL OFFER

DEALING WITH LONELINESS - $ 7.00

"Dealing With Loneliness"

By: SideKick

Dealing With Loneliness, while self explanatory, is one of the biggest problems for singles. This eBook is a quick and easy guide to tackling this problem and is a must read for all.

** Published 2007 **

Personality Types and Dating Guide - by SideKick
http://datingtorelating.com/inc/sdetail/3386
Reg. Price: ~~$20.00~~
Sale Price: $7.00
Save: $13.00

PERSONALITY TYPES AND DATING GUIDE- $ 7.00

"Personality Quadrant's Dating Guide"

By: SideKick

Personality Quadrant's Dating Guide is a fun-filled, light-hearted guide on how to get a good date by understanding yourself as well as understanding and interpreting how your date will behave based on his or her personality type!

** Published 2007 **

Guide To Adult Dating - by Dr. Dating
http://datingtorelating.com/inc/sdetail/3391
Reg. Price: ~~$20.00~~
Sale Price: $7.00
Save: $13.00

SPECIAL OFFER

GUIDE TO ADULT DATING - $ 7.00

**** Published 2006 ****

Guide To Adult Dating

If you're tired of the normal dating routines of going out for coffee or dinner with someone you just met in a bar, you might want to try a *spicier* style of dating. Adult dating may just be the thing to kick your sex life into high gear. It's for anyone who wants to explore the extent of their sexuality, bring their fantasies to life, or try something new. With Dr. Dating's "Guide to Adult Dating", you can venture into the highly coveted world of sexy adult dates.

Great Tips For Dating Success - by Dr. Dating

http://datingtorelating.com/inc/sdetail/3393

g. Price: ~~$20.00~~
Sale Price: $7.00
Save: $13.00

SPECIAL OFFER

GREAT TIPS FOR DATING SUCCESS - $ 7.00

Great Tips For Dating Success

Whether you're looking for a fun, casual dating experience or a powerful romantic encounter, Dr. Dating's *Great Tips for Dating Success* is just the guide you need. This guide was written and researched by Dr. Dating himself, to help people from all walks of life to find and enjoy great dates. This eBook has all the hot tips and tricks that will help increase your dating success.

**** NEW 2007 Version ****

---

5 Steps To Online Dating Success - by SideKick
http://datingtorelating.com/inc/sdetail/3385

Reg. Price: ~~$20.00~~
Sale Price: $7.00
Save: $13.00

SPECIAL OFFER

5 STEPS TO ONLINE DATING SUCCESS - $ 7.00

"5 Steps To Online Dating Success"

By: SideKick

-What You Need to Know About Online Dating First!
-What Makes Online Dating So Different?
-Getting Started
-Making Yourself Look Like A Million Dollars

**** Published 2007 ****

Guide To Online Dating - by Dr. Dating

http://datingtorelating.com/inc/sdetail/3394

Reg. Price: ~~$20.00~~

Sale Price: $7.00

Save: $13.00

SPECIAL OFFER

GUIDE TO ONLINE DATING - $ 7.00

** NEW 2007 Version **

Guide To Online Dating

Be honest - the single life can be depressing sometimes. You may try to find dates in bars, ask your friends to hook you up with someone, or even try dating services. If you don't' seem to have any success, you might find yourself giving up. But there's probably one dating frontier you haven't tried - online dating. More and more people all over the world are increasing their dating chances through the opportunities offered on the internet. With Dr. Dating's *Guide to Online Dating*, you can use the internet to give your dating life a complete makeover!

The Ultimate Man's Guide To Online Dating - by Dr. Dating
http://datingtorelating.com/inc/sdetail/3392

Reg. Price: ~~$20.00~~
Sale Price: $7.00
Save: $13.00

SPECIAL OFFER

THE ULTIMATE MAN'S GUIDE TO ONLINE DATING - $ 7.00

The Ultimate Man's Guide to Online Dating

Ever feel like you're meeting the wrong women? Have you dated around and found that you're looking for something more casual while your date wants a marriage? Or do you simply get nervous in front of an attractive girl? Trust me, we've all been there. Sometimes we'd rather hang out with the guys and watch a football game rather than risk the frustration of going out with women you don't want to see again. There's a better world of women out there - and Dr. Dating has written the perfect dating guide for you!

**** Published 2007 ****

A Teenager's Guide To Dating - by SideKick

http://datingtorelating.com/inc/sdetail/3388

Reg. Price: ~~$20.00~~
Sale Price: $7.00
Save: $13.00

SPECIAL OFFER

A TEENAGER'S GUIDE TO DATING - $ 7.00

"A Teenager's Guide To Dating"

By: SideKick

This is a comprehensive 128 page eBook written for Teenagers and the Adults who care about them. This eBook covers every aspect of teenage dating. A must for Teenagers and their Parents alike.

** Published 2007 **

How I Got 700 Dates In One Year - Mr. L. Rx

http://datingtorelating.com/inc/sdetail/3396

Reg. Price: ~~$20.00~~
Sale Price: $7.00
Save: $13.00

SPECIAL OFFER

"How I got over 700 dates in one year (and 2500 women's phone numbers)" - $7.00

Why Settle for doubling your dating when you can 10 x it?

Made in the USA
Charleston, SC
24 January 2012